MW00437298

Presented to

....

From

....

Date

....

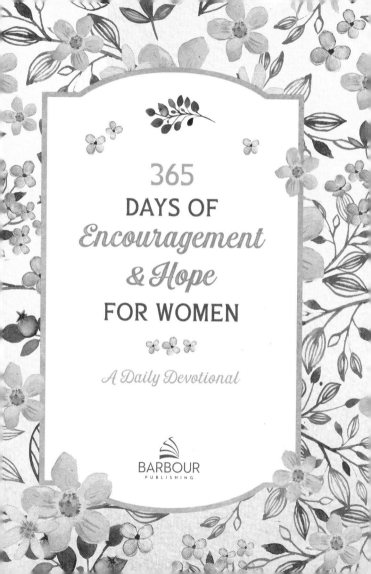

365
DAYS OF
Encouragement
& Hope
FOR WOMEN

A Daily Devotional

BARBOUR
PUBLISHING

© 2015 by Barbour Publishing, Inc.

ISBN 978-1-64352-896-0

Compiled by Kathy Shutt.

Our mission is to inspire the world with the life-changing message of the Bible.

Printed in China.

EVERYDAY
Encouragement & Hope

*I pray that God, the source of hope,
will fill you completely with joy and
peace because you trust in him.*
ROMANS 15:13 NLT

This lovely daily devotional offers just-right-sized readings that are a perfect fit for your busy lifestyle. These 365 devotional readings feature themes that are important to your heart—including faith, friendship, joy, love, rest, trust, peace, security, and dozens more. As you move through the pages of *365 Days of Encouragement and Hope for Women*, you'll be comforted and inspired every day of the year as you experience the refreshing peace and assurance that can only be found through an intimate relationship with the Master Creator.

DAY 1
Dancing in the Puddles

And so, Lord, where do I put my hope?
My only hope is in you.
PSALM 39:7 NLT

They say you can tell a lot about a person's foundation of hope by the way she handles a rainy day. Does she turn into a Gloomy Gussy, wailing, "Oh, woe is me. . ." or does she make the best of a bad situation? A hope-filled person will realize that abundant life in Christ isn't about simply enduring the storm but also about learning to dance in the puddles. So grab your galoshes, and let's boogie!

DAY 2
God's Plan

My dear brothers, take note of this:
Everyone should be quick to listen, slow to
speak and slow to become angry.
JAMES 1:19 NIV

God gives good advice on anger. Often, if we listen carefully and hold our tongues, we don't become angry in the first place. Good communication forestalls a lot of emotional trauma. Hurt emotions often cause us to speak words we regret, simply making the problem worse. So when we feel tempted to anger, let's stop, listen, and hold our tongues for a while. That's God's plan for more peaceful relationships.

DAY 3
Walking Faith

*"Be strong and courageous, and act; do not
fear nor be dismayed, for the LORD God, my God,
is with you. He will not fail you nor forsake you."*

1 CHRONICLES 28:20 NASB

What a life verse! What a creed to live by! We
are assured that our God will never leave us or
forsake us. We draw strength and courage from
this assurance and are then able to act; to share
our faith boldly—without fear—because we are
never alone. The Lord God—our God—is with us.

DAY 4

In His Hands

Do not be anxious about anything, but in every situation, by prayer and petition, with thanksgiving, present your requests to God.

PHILIPPIANS 4:6 NIV

Need a sure cure for anxiety? Start praying. As you trust that God has your best interests at heart, no matter what situation you face, His peace can replace concern. God says there's nothing you need to worry about. Just put all your troubles in His hands, and He who rules the universe yet knows each hair on your head will see that everything works out right. Are you ready to trust now?

DAY 5
Interior Decorator

You, O Lord, are a shield about me, my glory,
and the One who lifts my head.

Psalm 3:3 nasb

Have you ever caught a glimpse of yourself reflected in a window and were shocked at the hangdog image you unwittingly portrayed? Slumped shoulders, drooping head, defeated expression? You can straighten your posture and adjust your face, but if the change doesn't come from the inside out, it won't stick. God is our Interior Decorator. Only He can provide that inner joy that projects outward and lifts our heads. Invite Him in to work on your place.

DAY 6
God Is in Control

*"Who of you by being worried can
add a single hour to his life?"*
Matthew 6:27 nasb

What does worry gain us? It can't change the
length of our days, except to decrease the health
of our bodies. Ultimately, worry is the most self-
defeating thing we can engage in. Besides, why
should we give in to concern when God controls
our lives? He will always set us on the right path,
so we don't have to agonize over life's details.

DAY 7
Designer Label

We wish that each of you would always be eager to show how strong and lasting your hope really is.
HEBREWS 6:11 CEV

Our behavior is always on display and, like it or not, we are judged by our actions. . .and inactions. Without an explanation for our behavior—that we're motivated by faith to be Christlike—people will make up their own ideas: her mama taught her right; she was just born nice; she acts sweet so everyone will like her. Isn't it better to be up-front and give credit to the One we're emulating? Wear the label of your Designer proudly.

DAY 8
Blessing Others

We work hard with our own hands.
When we are cursed, we bless;
when we are persecuted, we endure it.
1 CORINTHIANS 4:12 NIV

God gave Paul many blessings, and the apostle passed them on, even if the recipients didn't seem to really deserve them. Those who cursed him (and they were, no doubt, many) did not receive a cursing in return. Instead, Paul tried to bless them. Do we follow the apostle's example? When we are cursed by the words of others, what is our response?

DAY 9
Inside-Out Love

*God has made everything
beautiful for its own time.*
ECCLESIASTES 3:11 NLT

Beauty is a concern of every woman to some degree. We worry about hair, makeup, weight, fashions. But real beauty can only come from God's inside-out love. Once we are able to finally comprehend His infinite and extravagant love for us—despite our flat feet and split ends—our heart glow will reflect radiant beauty from the inside out. Only when we feel truly loved are we free to be truly lovely.

DAY 10

Hold On to Hope

The prospect of the righteous is joy,
but the hopes of the wicked come to nothing.
PROVERBS 10:28 NIV

Trusting in Jesus gave you new life and hope for eternity. So how do you respond when life becomes dark and dull? Does hope slip away? When no obviously great spiritual works are going on, do not assume God has deserted you. Hold on to Him even more firmly and trust. He will keep His promises. Truly, what other option do you have? Without Him, hope disappears.

DAY 11
Granter of Dreams

*Hope deferred makes the heart sick,
but a dream fulfilled is a tree of life.*
PROVERBS 13:12 NLT

As a teenager, I dreamed of one day writing a book. But life intervened, and I became a wife, mother, occupational therapist, and piano teacher. My writing dream was shelved. Twenty-five years later, after my youngest chick flew the coop, God's still, small voice whispered, "It's time." Within five years, the Granter of Dreams delivered over seventy articles and nine book contracts. What's your dream? Be brave and take the first step.

DAY 12
A Godly Example

*"Let the little children come to Me,
and do not forbid them; for of such
is the kingdom of heaven."*
MATTHEW 19:14 NKJV

On earth, Jesus loved children. He never shut them out. Though their youth gave them little credence in Israel, He saw the faith potential in them. Certainly the children loved Jesus too for His kindheartedness. Do we shut children out of our lives because we are too busy or have more "important" things on our minds? Then we need to take an example from Jesus. For a new take on God's kingdom, spend time with a child today.

DAY 13
Everyday Blessings

*But the eyes of the LORD are on those who
fear him, on those whose hope
is in his unfailing love.*

<small>PSALM 33:18 NIV</small>

The Lord of all creation is watching our every moment and wants to fill us with His joy. He often interrupts our lives with His blessings: butterflies dancing in sunbeams, dew-touched spiderwebs, cotton candy clouds, and glorious crimson sunsets. The beauty of His creation reassures us of His unfailing love and fills us with hope. But it is up to us to take the time to notice.

DAY 14
God of Comfort

[God] comforts us in all our troubles, so that we
can comfort those in any trouble with the
comfort we ourselves receive from God.
2 CORINTHIANS 1:4 NIV

When you hurt, God offers you comfort. No trouble is so large or so small that He will not help. But when you have received His strength for the trouble at hand, do you share it in turn? Comfort isn't meant to be hidden away, but passed on to those in a similar need. As part of the body of Christ, we—the church—should be sharing the knowledge that God cares for and strengthens all His children.

DAY 15
Stop the Roller Coaster

*Why am I discouraged? Why is my heart
so sad? I will put my hope in God!*
PSALM 43:5 NLT

For women, ruts of depression are often caused by careening hormones. Rampaging hormones can cause us to spend countless hours weeping without knowing why—or bite someone's head off, lose precious sleep, or sprout funky nervous habits. Knowing that this hormonally crazed state is only temporary, we must intentionally place our hope in tomorrow and pray that God will turn the downside up!

DAY 16
Look to the Shepherd

The LORD is my shepherd,
I lack nothing.
PSALM 23:1 NIV

No matter what your physical circumstances, if Jesus is your Shepherd, you never have to want spiritually. No matter what the world throws at you, you can be at peace. No fear overcomes those who follow the Shepherd as their King. He guides them through every trial, leading them faithfully into an eternity with Him.

Are you lacking contentment today? Look to the Shepherd for peace.

DAY 17

My Refuge

God is our refuge and strength,
always ready to help in times of trouble.

PSALM 46:1 NLT

What is your quiet place? The place you go to get away from the fray, to chill out, think, regroup, and gain perspective? Mine is a hammock nestled beneath a canopy of oaks in my backyard. . . nobody around but birds, squirrels, an occasional wasp, God, and me. There I can pour out my heart to my Lord, hear His comforting voice, and feel His strength refresh me. We all need a quiet place. God, our refuge, will meet us there.

DAY 18
Watchful Love

*I have learned in whatever
state I am, to be content.*
PHILIPPIANS 4:11 NKJV

Paul wasn't writing about a grit-your-teeth kind
of contentment. He had learned to trust deeply
in God for all his needs, so the apostle did not
worry about future events. His strength lay in
God, who cared for his every need, even when
churches forgot him.

We too can be content in Jesus. If the boss
doesn't give us a raise or an unexpected bill comes
in, He knows it. Nothing escapes His watchful
love in our lives.

DAY 19
Stinkin' Thinkin'

*Let us be sober, having put on the breastplate
of faith and love, and as a helmet,
the hope of salvation.*
1 THESSALONIANS 5:8 NASB

Women's hats aren't as popular as they once were, but you wouldn't know it by my closet. I love accessorizing with a perky hat to make a statement, to disguise a bad hair day, or to keep my brain from sautéing in the sizzling Florida sun. The Bible says we need to protect our minds from bad spiritual rays too. Nasty input produces nasty output: stinkin' thinkin'. When we're tempted to input a questionable movie or book, let's don our salvation helmets and say, "No way!"

DAY 20
Our Hope

God raised him from the dead, freeing him from the agony of death, because it was impossible for death to keep its hold on him.

ACTS 2:24 NIV

Death could not grasp Jesus, the sinless One who died for the guilty. Though it clings to sinful beings, it had no claim on God's Son. Jesus is our only hope. Though sin deserves death, God's compassion made a way to free us from its agonies. When we give our poor, mortal lives to Jesus, we rise in Him, sharing His eternal life.

DAY 21

Redeeming Pain

I may have fallen, but I will get up;
I may be sitting in the dark,
but the LORD is my light.

MICAH 7:8 CEV

"Life is pain, Highness. Anyone who says differently is selling something." This memorable line from the movie *The Princess Bride* rings true. Pain is inevitable in life, but God can use it for redemptive purposes. Pain can knock us down, cast us into darkness, and make us feel defeated. But it's only as debilitating as we allow it to be. We will get up again; we will learn, adapt, and grow through redeeming pain.

DAY 22
God's Promise

*This is the promise that He
has promised us—eternal life.*
1 JOHN 2:25 NKJV

The promise of eternal life comes straight from God. Those who receive Jesus into their hearts do not end their existence when they stop breathing. Their last breath on earth is merely a precursor of life in eternity with Jesus. Today you miss the one you lost, and your heart aches. But in eternity, you will be reunited and will share the joys of death conquered by the Savior. Until you meet again, simply trust in His unfailing promise.

Maid of Honor

*For I fully expect and hope that. . .
my life will bring honor to Christ,
whether I live or die.*

PHILIPPIANS 1:20 NLT

Honor. A word not as respected in our society as it once was. In these days of suggestive attire, cohabitation without marriage, and tolerance for every behavior imaginable, it's hard to remember what honor means. As Christians, our hope and expectation is to honor Christ with our lives—especially in the details—because we are the only reflection of Jesus some people might ever see.

DAY 24
The Only Way

"I am the way and the truth and the life.
No one comes to the Father
except through me."
John 14:6 niv

Plenty of people doubt Jesus. But those who have accepted Him as their Savior need not wallow in uncertainty. His Spirit speaks to ours, moment by moment, if we will only listen. He tells us God has shown us the way; we need not seek another path or truth. No other road leads to God. For a vibrant Christian life, we simply need to continue down the highway we're traveling with Jesus.

DAY 25
It'll Be All Right

Our comfort is abundant through Christ.
2 Corinthians 1:5 nasb

As children, there's no greater comfort than running to Mommy or Daddy and hearing, "It'll be all right." As adults, when we're frightened, dismayed, or dispirited, we yearn to run to enveloping arms for the same comfort. Abba Father—Papa God—is waiting with open arms to offer us loving comfort in our times of need. If we listen closely, we'll hear His still, small voice speak to our hearts: "It'll be all right, My child."

DAY 26
Compassion

Be merciful to those who doubt.
JUDE 22 NIV

If you've ever doubted (as we all have), you can understand why this verse is in the Bible. If well-meaning folks attacked you for your uncertainty, it probably didn't help—they just made you more nervous.

When questions enter our minds, we need someone encouraging to come alongside us and provide answers, not a critic who wants to condemn our feelings. Knowing that, we also need compassion for other doubters. May we be the merciful ones who aid those doubting hearts.

DAY 27
I Am His

*My health may fail, and my spirit may grow weak,
but God remains the strength of my
heart; he is mine forever.*

<small>PSALM 73:26 NLT</small>

My dear friend was dying of an inoperable brain tumor. Mother of three, 48-year-old Sherill could no longer walk or care for herself, yet her voice was filled with hope as she gazed unwaveringly into my eyes and quoted this verse. She added something very significant at the end that I'll hold close to my heart and draw strength from when my time comes: "He is mine forever. . .and I am His."

DAY 28
Always Secure

Your throne was established long ago;
you are from all eternity.

PSALM 93:2 NIV

There was never a moment when God did not exist. No scrap of time or eternity came into being without Him, and nothing escapes His powerful reign. That's good news for His children. For whatever we face, now or in our heavenly abode, we know our Father is in control. No spiritual warfare or earthly disaster lies beyond His plan. No wickedness of Satan can take Him by surprise. Ours is the eternal Lord, who has loved us from the start. In Him, we are always secure.

DAY 29
Increasing Visibility

"Where then is my hope?"
JOB 17:15 NIV

On hectic days when fatigue takes its toll, when we feel like cornless husks, hope disappears. When hurting people hurt people, and we're in the line of fire, hope vanishes. When ideas fizzle, efforts fail; when we throw the spaghetti against the wall and nothing sticks, hope seems lost. But we must remember it's only temporary. The mountaintop isn't gone just because it's obscured by fog. Visibility will improve tomorrow, and hope will rise.

DAY 30
Unchanging

Your word, LORD, is eternal;
it stands firm in the heavens.
PSALM 119:89 NIV

The Word of God never changes. The Father's commands do not alter, and neither does Jesus, the Word made flesh, or His promise of salvation. Those who trust in Him are secure as the Lord Himself, for He does not change, and none of His promises pass away unfulfilled. The eternal Lord and all He commands stand firm. To gain eternity, simply receive Christ as your Savior; then trust in Him.

DAY 31
Wag More

*I am not complaining about having too
little. I have learned to be satisfied
with whatever I have.*
PHILIPPIANS 4:11 CEV

I oozed envy as writer buddies received awards,
broke sales records, and snagged lucrative
contracts. What about me? Where were my
accolades? It had always been enough to know
I was following God's chosen path for me, but
suddenly all I could do was complain. I wanted
more.

Then God sent me a sign. Actually, it was a
bumper sticker on a passing car: Wag More, Bark
Less. Message received. . .with a smile.

DAY 32
Pure Delight

You make known to me the path of life;
you will fill me with joy in your presence,
with eternal pleasures at your right hand.

PSALM 16:11 NIV

Rejoicing in God? Those who do not know Jesus cannot imagine it. You have to know Jesus to delight in His presence, just as you cannot enjoy a friend until you come to know each other and enjoy companionship. But knowing and loving God brings us, His children, joy in His presence and the prospect of undefined pleasures at His side. Are you prepared to share those joys with Jesus for eternity?

DAY 33
Lord of the Dance

Remember your promise to me;
it is my only hope.
PSALM 119:49 NLT

The Bible contains many promises from God:
He will protect us (Proverbs 1:33), comfort us
(2 Corinthians 1:5), help in our times of trouble
(Psalm 46:1), and encourage us (Isaiah 40:29).
The word *encourage* comes from the root phrase
"to inspire courage." Like an earthly father
encouraging his daughter from backstage as
her steps falter during her dance recital, our
Papa God wants to inspire courage in us, if we
only look to Him.

DAY 34
He Never Fails

*If we are faithless, he remains faithful,
for he cannot disown himself.*
2 TIMOTHY 2:13 NIV

Sometimes our faith fails, but Jesus never does. When we change for the worse, slip, or make a mistake, He is still the same faithful God He's always been. Though we may falter, He cannot. If we give in to the tempter's wiles, let us turn again to the faithful One. If we have trusted in Him, we can turn to Him for renewed forgiveness. His own faithfulness will not allow Him to deny us.

DAY 35
Light My Fire

If God is for us, who can be against us?
ROMANS 8:31 NIV

Some days it feels as if the entire world is conspiring to make us as miserable as possible. Your spouse is crabby, the kids forget to mention the four dozen cupcakes they volunteered you to bake for today, traffic jams, your boss is on the rampage, your coworkers are in nasty moods, you forgot to defrost dinner, the car overheats again. But our God is King of the Universe, and He's on our side. Girl, if that doesn't light your fire, the wood's wet.

DAY 36

Perfection

*His works are perfect, and all his ways
are just. A faithful God who does no
wrong, upright and just is he.*

DEUTERONOMY 32:4 NIV

Many unbelievers, or even weakening believers living in crisis, complain that God is unfair. But Moses, who suffered much for God's people, knew better than that. God is always perfect, faithful, and just—it's rebellious humanity that lacks these qualities.

We can have faith in God's perfection. He's never failed His people yet, though they have often been false. Trust in Him today. As He led His people to the Promised Land, He'll lead you home to Himself.

DAY 37
Acing the Test

*Always be ready to give an answer when
someone asks you about your hope.*

1 Peter 3:15 CEV

Remember algebra tests in high school? Instant
sweat and heart palpitations. You dreaded going
into them unprepared. You wanted to have
answers ready so you wouldn't be left with
saliva drooling from your gaping mouth when
questioned. The Bible says we should be prepared
when someone asks about the hope within us—
the hope they couldn't help but notice radiating
from our souls. The answer scores an A+ for all
eternity: Jesus!

DAY 38
Praise Him

Let them praise the name of the LORD,
for His name alone is exalted; His glory
is above the earth and heaven.
PSALM 148:13 NKJV

Trusting Jesus gives you a spectacular view of God's power. His work in your life increasingly opens your eyes to this glorious King who loves you. But those who do not know Him cannot praise Him. They are thoroughly blind to the glories of the One whom they have denied. Yet in the end, His glory will be apparent even to them. Whom do you follow—the glorious One or mere humans?

DAY 39
Chef d'oeuvre

Be strong and let your heart take courage,
all you who hope in the LORD.
PSALM 31:24 NASB

Identical eggs can be turned into greasy fried egg sandwiches or an exquisite soufflé. The difference is how much beating they endure.

When life seems to be beating us down, we must remember that we are a masterpiece in progress. The mixing, slicing, and dicing may feel brutal at times, but our Lord has offered us His courage and strength to endure until He is ready to unveil the chef d'oeuvre.

DAY 40
Building a House

The wise woman builds her house, but the foolish pulls it down with her hands.

PROVERBS 14:1 NKJV

Did you know you can build a house? God says so. No, you won't use mortar, brick, and wood. But every Christian woman has the ability to build up her family with her wisdom, industry, and righteousness. Her faithful Christian character blesses those in her home. Today, are you building your house or tearing it down? Seek God, and He will help you make it strong.

DAY 41
Superglue Faith

In Him, you also, after listening to the message of truth, the gospel of your salvation—having also believed, you were sealed in Him with the Holy Spirit of promise.

EPHESIANS 1:13 NASB

Remember the old commercial that depicted a construction worker dangling in midair, the top of his helmet bonded by superglue to a horizontal beam? Faith is like superglue. We cling to our God, our foundation, our beam. As believers, we are sealed in Christ, and the bond cannot be undone. Through prayer in times of despair, our faith is strengthened and becomes waterproof, pressure-resistant, and unbreakable.

DAY 42
Parents

"Honor your father and your mother, that your days may be long upon the land."

EXODUS 20:12 NKJV

When we honor our parents, we may not spend much time in the Promised Land, but God will bless us. Treating Mom and Dad well improves our relationships with them and gives our family security. As we treat our children's grandparents well, we model the actions of adult children, and our children are more likely to treat us well too.

Our Father God has special blessings for those of us who respect our parents. Whether it's Holy Land property or deeper love, He gives us just what we need.

DAY 43
Keep Breathing, Sister!

As long as we are alive, we still have hope,
just as a live dog is better off than a dead lion.
ECCLESIASTES 9:4 CEV

Isn't this a tremendous scripture? At first glance, the ending elicits a chuckle. But consider the truth it contains: regardless of how powerful, regal, or intimidating a lion is, when he's dead, he's dead. But the living—you and I—still have hope. Limitless possibilities! Hope for today and for the future. Although we may be as lowly dogs, fresh, juicy bones abound. As long as we're breathing, it's not too late!

DAY 44

Appreciation for Mothers

Her children arise and call her blessed;
her husband also, and he praises her.

PROVERBS 31:28 NIV

Wouldn't every woman like to receive this kind of praise? A few do. Though we all need praise for a job well done, many families forget to encourage their members. When we have followed God faithfully, it shows in our lives, but we still value others' appreciation. Has a Christian mother been a wonderful influence on your life? She'd probably like to know that. Feel free to share that praise with others too.

DAY 45
It's a Mystery

*This is the day which the LORD has made;
let us rejoice and be glad in it.*

PSALM 118:24 NASB

Let's face it, girls, some mornings our rejoicing lasts only until the toothpaste drips onto our new shirt or the toast sets off the fire alarm. But the mystery of Jesus-joy is that it's not dependent on rosy circumstances. If we, after cleaning the shirt and scraping the toast, intentionally give our day to the Lord, He will infuse it with His joy. Things look much better through Jesus-joy contact lenses!

DAY 46
Fear Will Flee

Do not be afraid of sudden terror, nor of trouble from the wicked when it comes; for the LORD will be your confidence, and will keep your foot from being caught.

PROVERBS 3:25–26 NKJV

What do you have to fear, with God as your confidence? He protects you from being snared like a wild animal by the world's troubles. With His hand over you, no sudden event or evildoer's plot can destroy you. Give Him your confidence, and fear will flee.

DAY 47

Going the Distance

*[David]. . .chose five smooth stones from the
stream. . .and, with his sling in his hand,
approached the Philistine.*

1 SAMUEL 17:40 NIV

That little dude David had no intention of backing
down from his fight until it was finished. Notice
he picked up five rocks, not just one. He was
prepared to go the distance against his giant.
He fully expected God to make him victorious,
but he knew it wouldn't be easy.

So you've used your first rock against your
giant. Maybe even your second. Don't give up.
Keep reloading your sling and go the distance.
Victory is sweet!

DAY 48
Fearing God

In the fear of the LORD there is strong confidence,
and His children will have a place of refuge.
PROVERBS 14:26 NKJV

There is only one right kind of fear—the fear of God. Not that we need to cower before Him, but we must respect and honor Him and His infinite power. Those who love Him also rightly fear Him. But those who fear God need fear nothing else. He is their refuge, the Protector whom nothing can bypass. Fear God, and you are safe.

DAY 49
Top Off My Tank

"My grace is sufficient for you, for my power is made perfect in weakness."

2 Corinthians 12:9 niv

There is no weaker vessel than a bedraggled mother at 6 a.m., staring into a bathroom mirror after another rough night. She's trying to decide if the dark smudges beneath her eyes are yesterday's grape jelly when she suddenly realizes she's brushing her hair with her toothbrush. Yep, we are a sisterhood of slightly sagging spiritual warriors, but we can depend on God to power our weak vessels. And He is able.

Secure in the Father

*The Spirit you received does not make you slaves,
so that you live in fear again; rather, the Spirit you
received brought about your adoption to sonship.
And by him we cry, "Abba, Father."*
ROMANS 8:15 NIV

As part of God's family, you need never dread anything. He who rules the universe adopted you. Since your loving Father no longer condemns you for sin, panic need not rule your life. Fear no retribution, because your elder brother Jesus shed His blood for you, covering every sin. God's child always remains secure in her Abba, "Daddy."

DAY 51
Heavyweight

*This hope is like a firm
and steady anchor for our souls.*
HEBREWS 6:19 CEV

Julia and Mark anchored their sailboat to do a little reef exploring while they went diving. When they surfaced, the boat was a speck on the horizon. It had drifted more than a half mile because their anchor was too light.

Hope in Christ is an anchor for our souls. But if the anchor isn't weighted by firm and steady faith, we may drift in strong currents of doubt, problems, and disillusionment. Weigh your anchor today.

DAY 52
Blessing of Forgiveness

[Your] sins have been forgiven
on account of his name.
1 JOHN 2:12 NIV

Who could do something wonderful enough to earn God's forgiveness? No human work can buy it. God forgives because of who He is, not because of who we are or what we do. That's encouraging, because we can't earn forgiveness by our own perfection. Instead, forgiveness becomes the great blessing of our Christian life that makes living for Jesus possible. We obey God to show our appreciation, not to gain entry into His kingdom.

DAY 53
A Perfect Fit

The LORD is good to those whose hope is in him, to the one who seeks him.

LAMENTATIONS 3:25 NIV

Seeking God is, for some, like a child groping in a dark room for the light switch. She knows it's there, she just can't seem to put her fingers on it. Some search for God all their lives, trying on various religions like pairs of shoes. This one pinches. That one chafes. But we must bypass religious fluff for the heart of the matter: Jesus. The only way to God is through faith in Christ (John 14:6). Suddenly, the shoe fits!

DAY 54

An End to Mourning

*"Blessed are those who mourn,
for they will be comforted."*
MATTHEW 5:4 NIV

How often do we think of mourning as a good thing? But when it comes to sin, it is. Those who sorrow over their own sinfulness will turn to God for forgiveness. When He willingly responds to their repentance, mourning ends. Comforted by God's pardon, transformed sinners celebrate— and joyous love for Jesus replaces sorrow.

DAY 55
Roots

"There is hope for your future,"
declares the LORD, "and your children
will return to their own territory."
JEREMIAH 31:17 NASB

Prodigal. The word alone evokes an involuntary shudder.

Most of us know parents whose children have left home in the throes of rebellion. Some of us are those parents. After years of protecting and nurturing our children, heartache replaces harmony, panic supersedes pride. But the Great Peacemaker declares that prodigals will one day return to their roots. One of His greatest parables reinforces that hope (Luke 15).

DAY 56
Chosen Family

*There is a friend that
sticketh closer than a brother.*
PROVERBS 18:24 KJV

Family relationships range from the wonderful
to the disturbing, and we get whatever God gives
us. But we choose our friends based on common
interests and experiences. Often this "chosen
family" seems closer to us than siblings. Yet
neither clings closer than our elder brother Jesus.
He teaches us how to love blood relatives and
those we choose. No matter if we're related, when
we love in Him, that love sticks fast.

DAY 57
Legacy of Love

After all, when the Lord Jesus appears,
who else but you will give us hope and
joy and be like a glorious crown for us?
1 THESSALONIANS 2:19 CEV

The most hope-inspiring legacy we can pass on to the next generation is faith. What delight it is for us as women to plant and nurture seeds of faith in our children, knowing that at harvest they'll stand by our sides before the Lord Jesus! It's never too late to till the fertile soil of their hearts by our example of daily Bible reading, prayer, and dependence on our Savior.

DAY 58
Prayerful Giving

Give, and it shall be given unto you; good measure, pressed down. . .and running over.
LUKE 6:38 KJV

Need an example of how to give? Look to God. To those who give generously, He gives overflowing, abundant blessings.

In this fallen world, we need to be careful to whom we give support. Dishonest people or those who oppose God should not be our charitable choices. But many Christian ministries do good work and need our support. Faithful churches need our giving. As we donate prayerfully, God will bless us in return.

DAY 59

His Little Girls

Just as a father has compassion
on his children, so the LORD has
compassion on those who fear Him.

PSALM 103:13 NASB

Plagued with horrible recurring nightmares during my childhood, I remember the terror of waking up screaming, hair sweat-plastered to my face. Then like a candle in the darkness, my father would appear at my bedside, lie beside me, and gently rub my back until I fell asleep. Our heavenly Father is like that—tender, caring, protective. And He too responds when His little girls need comfort from His loving presence.

DAY 60
Want vs. Need

"Give us this day our daily bread."
MATTHEW 6:11 NKJV

Jesus tells us here to ask God for our daily needs, and we may do that frequently. Let's remember that even the smallest things, such as the bread we put on the table, come from God. Yet have we forgotten that all our food comes from our heavenly Father? God forgets nothing we need. So if we don't have steak instead of hamburgers, could it be because we want, but don't need, it?

DAY 61
Let the Sun Shine In

*"Come to me, all you who are weary and
burdened, and I will give you rest."*
MATTHEW 11:28 NIV

Nothing chokes hope like weariness. Day in and
day out, drudgery produces weariness of body,
heart, and soul. It feels like dark clouds have
obscured the sun and cast us into perpetual
shadow. But Jesus promised rest for our weary
souls, respite from our burdens, and healing for
our wounds. . .if we come to Him. The sun isn't
really gone, it's just hidden until the clouds roll
away.

DAY 62
Share His Love

"It is more blessed to give than to receive."
ACTS 20:35 NIV

Christmas has become a time of receiving—to the point where greed motivates more people than does blessing. But Paul reminds us that getting what we want is not the greatest blessing. We know that when we see the delight in a child's eyes at receiving a longed-for item. Our heavenly Father loves to see the same joy in our eyes when He helps us in less tangible ways. That's why He tells us to share His love with others.

DAY 63
No Wimps Here

For God has not given us a spirit of fear and timidity, but of power, love, and self-discipline.
2 TIMOTHY 1:7 NLT

Do you suffer paralysis by analysis? Are you so afraid of trying something new that you put it off until you can think it through. . .and end up doing nothing at all? Too much introspection creates inertia, and we abhor the ineffective wimps we become. Sisters, God never intended for us to be wimps. His power and love are available to replace our fear and infuse us with courage. Shake off that paralysis and get moving!

DAY 64

Compassion

A father to the fatherless, a defender of widows,
is God in his holy dwelling.

PSALM 68:5 NIV

God's love is very tender toward those who hurt.
Children who have lost their fathers and women
who have lost their husbands can count on His
compassion. When we lose a loved one, do we
focus on the Father's gentleness? We are more
likely to complain that He did not extend life than
to praise Him for His care. But when we feel the
most pain, we also receive the largest portion of
God's comfort. What hurts His children hurts
Him too.

DAY 65
When I'm Baaad

*"I am the good shepherd; I know my own sheep,
and they know me, just as my Father
knows me and I know the Father."*

JOHN 10:14–15 NLT

Ever spent much time around sheep? They're really self-centered. All they think about is eating, sleeping, and avoiding conflict. But one good thing about sheep is that they'll drop everything and respond to their shepherd's voice. Not anybody else's voice, just the familiar tones of their own shepherd. This little ewe wants to recognize and respond to her beloved Shepherd's voice too. How about you, ewe?

DAY 66
Simple Words

Strengthen those who have tired hands,
and encourage those who have weak knees.
ISAIAH 35:3 NLT

A simple word of encouragement or act of kindness can live in memory for years and even a lifetime. You may think someone who holds a high position or appears to have everything under control doesn't need any encouragement, but you never know how unsure of herself or emotionally frayed she's feeling inside. Perhaps your "Wonderful job!" is the confidence booster she's longing to hear. It's possible your thumbs-up is all it will take for someone to know that others notice, understand, and care.

DAY 67
Tolerance Isn't Enough

"In his name the nations will put their hope."
MATTHEW 12:21 NIV

In the summer of 2000, my husband and I toured the Holy Land. Our Israeli guide assured us that there was no safer place than Jerusalem, for people of numerous faiths—Muslim, Jewish, Christian, Hindu—had learned tolerance as the key to living together peaceably. Yet tension was as evident as the armed guards on every street corner. Violence erupted three months later with the first bus bombings. Our only hope for peace is Jehovah.

DAY 68
Children of God

Because you are his sons, God sent the Spirit of his Son into our hearts, the Spirit who calls out, "Abba, Father."

GALATIANS 4:6 NIV

God draws His children near, connecting them firmly to Himself through the Son and the Holy Spirit. There is no division in the Godhead when it comes to loving God's adopted children. With the Spirit, we call out, "Abba, Daddy," to the Holy One who loved us enough to call us to Himself despite our sin. Through Jesus' sacrifice and the Spirit's work, God the Father cleanses us and opens communications so we can follow Him truly.

DAY 69
Questions and Answers

*And the Scriptures were written to teach
and encourage us by giving us hope.*
ROMANS 15:4 CEV

What do you do when facing a perplexing problem? Ask a family member? Consult a friend? Turn to the Internet?

God's Word is brimming with answers to life's difficulties, yet it's often the last place we turn. God speaks to us today through the lives of trusting Abraham, brokenhearted Ruth, runaway Jonah, courageous Esther, female leader Deborah in a male-dominated society, beaten-down Job, double-crossing Peter, and Paul, who proved people can change.

DAY 70
Stand Firm

The LORD has become my fortress,
and my God the rock in whom I take refuge.
PSALM 94:22 NIV

Are you under attack by friends, family, or coworkers? If it comes because of your obedience to the Lord, stand firm in the face of their comments. He will defend you. If you face harsh words or nasty attitudes, remain kind, and He will assist you. Should your boss do you wrong, don't worry. Those who are against a faithful Christian are also against Him, and God will somehow make things right.

DAY 71

Hit the Mats

Blessed are those whose help is the God of Jacob,
whose hope is in the LORD their God.
PSALM 146:5 NIV

Wrestled with God lately? We all do at one time or another. The Genesis 32 account of Jacob's Almighty wrestling match reassures us that God is not offended when we beat on His chest and shout, "Why?" He understands that we must sometimes wrestle out the mysteries of our faith. Wrestling with his Lord was a turning point for Jacob—he got a new name (Israel) and a new perspective. God is ready to do the same for us.

DAY 72
Our Refuge

The LORD Almighty is the one you are to regard as holy. . .he will be a holy place.
ISAIAH 8:13–14 NIV

When you live in awe of God—when He alone is Lord of your life—you have nothing to fear. If fears or enemies assail you, a place of refuge is always nearby. God never throws His children to the wolves. Instead, He protects them in His holy place. With Jesus as your Savior, you always have a peaceful place to go to.

DAY 73
Girlfriends

*And our hope for you is firm, because we know
that just as you share in our sufferings,
so also you share in our comfort.*

2 CORINTHIANS 1:7 NIV

Anne of Green Gables was right: bosom friends
are important. Girls need girlfriends. . .little girls
and grown-up girls alike. God wired us to need
each other, to yearn for the heart-bonding that
results from sharing sufferings, comfort, hugs,
and giggles. Nothing's wrong with men, of course,
but they don't make the same bosom friends as
girls. Have you thanked the Lord lately for your
soul sisters?

DAY 74
Receive His Strength

The LORD also will be a refuge for the oppressed,
a refuge in times of trouble.
PSALM 9:9 NKJV

The Psalms often speak of God as a refuge. Whether you face something large, like oppression, or something much smaller, He wants you to turn to Him in troublous times. Size does not matter, but your trust in Jesus does. Nothing you face is a shock to Him—He knows your troubles and has not deserted you. So, go to your refuge and take strength from Him.

DAY 75
Heaven's Bakery

*"Those who hope in me will
not be disappointed."*
ISAIAH 49:23 NIV

✿❀✿

As I stood in line ogling luscious pastries in the coffee shop's glass case, I asked the teenage clerk which she would suggest. Casting cornflower-blue eyes heavenward, she tapped her dainty chin with one finger before answering in a wistful voice. "I recommend the blueberry cheesecake. When I eat it, I hear angels." What higher recommendation is there? What greater hope have we than heaven? (Maybe they'll even serve blueberry cheesecake there!)

DAY 76
Loving Jesus

*Looking unto Jesus the author
and finisher of our faith.*
HEBREWS 12:2 KJV

God is writing a story of faith through your life.
What will it describe? Will it be a chronicle of
challenges overcome, like the Old Testament
story of Joseph? Or a near tragedy turned into
joy, like that of the prodigal son? Whatever your
account says, if you love Jesus, the end is never in
question. Those who love Him finish in heaven,
despite their trials on earth. The long, weary path
ends in His arms. Today, write a chapter in your
faithful narrative of God's love.

DAY 77
Beyond the Horizon

You will be rewarded for this;
your hope will not be disappointed.
PROVERBS 23:18 NLT

Have you ever traversed a long, winding road, unable to see your final destination? Perhaps you were surprised by twists and turns along the way or jarred by unexpected potholes. But you were confident that if you stayed on that road, you would eventually reach your destination. Likewise, God has mapped out our futures. The end of the road may disappear beyond the horizon, but we are assured that our destination will not be disappointing.

DAY 78
Spiritual Certainty

We live by faith, not by sight.
2 CORINTHIANS 5:7 NIV

There is more than one way of seeing. We view the world around us with our eyes, but by doing so, we don't apprehend all there is in life. Those things we "see" by faith cannot be envisioned by our physical eyes. That's why doubters disbelieve them. But when God speaks to our hearts, it is as real as if we'd viewed the truth plainly in front of us. Like Paul, though our eyes cannot see it, we have a spiritual certainty.

DAY 79

Kingdom-Purposed Friendship

"I tell you, use worldly wealth to gain friends for
yourselves, so that when it is gone, you will
be welcomed into eternal dwellings."

LUKE 16:9 NIV

There is a good way to use the things of the world, and Jesus describes it here. God has given us the wealth to share with others, making use of it to further God's kingdom. Though we may not have more than a pot of soup and some bread to offer, they can be the start of a kingdom-purposed friendship. What do you have that God can use this way?

DAY 80
Whom Do You Fear?

"I tell you, my friends, do not be afraid
of those who kill the body and after
that can do no more."

LUKE 12:4 NIV

Whom do you fear? If it's anyone other than God, take heart. You need not concern yourself with anything that person can do to you. Even those who can take your life can't change your eternal destination. So, if someone doesn't like your faith, don't sweat it. Put your trust in God and serve Him faithfully, and you need not fear.

DAY 81
Never Alone

I am convinced that nothing can ever separate us from God's love. Neither death nor life, neither angels nor demons, neither our fears for today nor our worries about tomorrow— not even the powers of hell can separate us from God's love.

ROMANS 8:38 NLT

I read a poll that said being alone is one of women's worst fears. When we experience loss, we sometimes feel that we're struggling all alone; that others around us can't possibly comprehend the scope of our fears, our worries, our pain. But the Bible says we're not alone, that nothing can separate us from our heavenly Father. He is right there beside us, loving us, offering His companionship when we have none.

DAY 82

Disconnect from the World

*Whosoever therefore will be a friend
of the world is the enemy of God.*
JAMES 4:4 KJV

There are good friendships and bad ones. When Christ becomes your best friend, other relationships may become distant. Old, carnal friendships no longer seem so attractive. Your lifestyles clash, and old friends become confused. But this separation is part of God's plan of holiness. Jesus disconnects you from the world and draws you close to His people—Christian friends who share your love for Him. Together you may reach out to those old friends for Jesus too.

DAY 83

Pure and Unspoiled

And everyone who has this hope fixed on Him purifies himself, just as He is pure.
1 JOHN 3:3 NASB

Don't you just love taking the first scoop of ice cream from a fresh half gallon? There's something about the smooth surface of unspoiled purity that satisfies the soul. It's the same with new jars of peanut butter, freshly fallen snow, or stretches of pristine, early morning beach sand. God looks at us that way—unblemished, pure, and unspoiled—through our faith and hope in Him. Allow that thought to bring a smile to your face today.

DAY 84
Getting What You Give

Whoever sows sparingly will also reap sparingly, and whoever sows generously will also reap generously.
2 CORINTHIANS 9:6 NIV

What you give is what you get. That's true in life, and it's also true spiritually. Anyone who tries to hold finances close will be letting go of spiritual blessings, while the person who shares generously gains in so many ways. It's hard to give up worldly treasures, but when you give in the name of Jesus, you will never run short.

DAY 85
The Palm of His Hand

If I ride the wings of the morning, if I dwell by the farthest oceans, even there your hand will guide me, and your strength will support me.

PSALM 139:9–10 NLT

Surf foamed around my ankles as I lifted the burgundy starfish, its pointed tips curled in taut contraction. "It's okay, little fellow, I'll help you," I crooned, gently cradling the sea creature stranded by the outgoing tide. Tiny tentacles tickled my palm as the starfish relaxed, safe and protected. Likewise, God's hand rescues, supports, and guides us to life-sustaining waters when we're stranded. We're safe in the palm of His hand.

DAY 86
Turn to Him

"I will be a Father to you, and you shall be My sons and daughters, says the LORD Almighty."
2 CORINTHIANS 6:18 NKJV

Only unconfessed sin can separate you from the Father. But God never desires such distance. He wants to draw near, like a loving Father who holds His child, provides for her, and helps her at every turn.

Though your earthly father was less than perfect, your heavenly Father is not. He heals your hurts, solves your problems, and offers His love at every turn. All you need to do is turn to Him in love.

DAY 87
Cherished Desire

God our Father loves us. He is kind and has given us eternal comfort and a wonderful hope.
2 THESSALONIANS 2:16 CEV

Webster's definition of hope: "to cherish a desire with expectation." In other words, yearning for something wonderful you expect to occur. Our hope in Christ is not just yearning for something wonderful, as in "I hope for a sunny beach day." It's a deep trust with roots that extend from the beginning of time to the infinite future. Our hope is not just the anticipation of heaven, but the expectation of a fulfilling life walking beside our Creator and best Friend.

DAY 88
Nothing Is Hidden

*Nothing in all creation
is hidden from God's sight.*
HEBREWS 4:13 NIV

Good or bad, nothing escapes God's notice. None of it is unknown to the Creator of the universe. And because He knows all, we can completely trust in God. He protects us from the wicked and supports the good in our lives because He knows just how both will touch us. When sorrow or trouble comes our way, we can count on His using it to benefit us—here and in eternity.

DAY 89
First Love

But you must stay deeply rooted and firm in your faith. You must not give up the hope you received when you heard the good news.
COLOSSIANS 1:23 CEV

Do you remember the day you turned your life over to Christ? Can you recall the flood of joy and hope that coursed through your veins? Ah, the wonder of first love. Like romantic love that deepens and broadens with passing years, our relationship with Jesus evolves into a river of faith that endures the test of time.

DAY 90
He Is Faithful

Blessed are those whose help is the God of
Jacob. . .the LORD. . .he remains faithful forever.
PSALM 146:5–6 NIV

You are not the only one who has experienced
God's faithfulness. Through the years, believers
have experienced His provision. Read Old
Testament accounts of those who have never seen
Him fail. Watch His acts in the New Testament
as He showed the church that it could trust Him.
God cannot fail His children, and He will not fail
you. Trust in the God of Jacob, and pass on your
testimony of His faithfulness.

DAY 91
Astounding Rescue

*Then I remember something that fills me
with hope. The LORD's kindness never fails!*
LAMENTATIONS 3:21–22 CEV

With our hectic lifestyles, pausing to remember
the past isn't something we do very often. But
perhaps we should. Then when doubts assault our
faith, fears threaten to devour us, and disaster
hovers like a dark cloud, we'll remember God's
past loving-kindnesses. Hope will triumph over
despair. Keeping a prayer journal is a wonderful
way to chronicle answered prayer. We'll always
remember the times when God's merciful hands
rescued us in astounding ways.

DAY 92
All-Powerful

God is our refuge and strength,
an ever-present help in trouble.
PSALM 46:1 NIV

When we face serious troubles, people often cannot provide the solution. Limited by human frailty, even the most generous of them can only help us so much. In every trouble, we have a greater asset if we believe in Jesus. Our all-powerful Creator offers protection from harm and strength for the longest trial. He always wants to come to our aid. Facing a trouble of any size? Turn to Him today.

DAY 93
Keeping Us in Stitches

The secret things belong to the LORD our God.
DEUTERONOMY 29:29 NIV

Have you ever noticed the messy underside of a needlepoint picture? Ugly knots, loose threads, and clashing colors appear random, without pattern. Yet if you turn it over, an exquisite, intricate design is revealed, each stitch blending to create a beautiful finished picture. Such is the fabric of our lives. The knots and loose threads may not make sense to us, but the Master Designer has a plan. The secret design belongs to Him.

DAY 94
Never Forgotten

*Who is like the LORD our God. . .who stoops down
to look on the heavens and the earth?*
PSALM 113:5–6 NIV

This all-powerful Lord, to whom the heavens and
earth are small, cares not just for your universe,
but for you. The verses that follow these describe
His love for even the humblest person. Though
you may face times of struggle, your awesome
Lord will never forget you. One day, as verse 8
of this psalm promises, even the humble can
sit with princes.

DAY 95

One Hunky Verse

To Him who is able to do far more abundantly
beyond all that we ask or think, according to
the power that works within us, to Him be
the glory. . .forever and ever. Amen.
EPHESIANS 3:20–21 NASB

Don't you just love the bigness of this verse? It
radiates with the enormity of God—that nothing
is beyond His scope or power. Read it aloud and
savor the words *far more abundantly.* Now repeat
"beyond all that we ask or think" three times,
pondering each word individually. Wow! If there
was ever a hunky verse to cast an attitude of
gratitude over our day, this is it. Yay, God!

DAY 96
Tender Love

This is love: not that we loved God,
but that he loved us and sent his Son as
an atoning sacrifice for our sins.

1 JOHN 4:10 NIV

We weren't sitting around thinking about loving God before He touched our lives. God began the process before we were even born. He sent His Son to bring us into communion with Him, and His Spirit drew us into a relationship with Him. We respond to God's overwhelmingly tender love when we invite Jesus into our lives. Even so, many years of obedience show our gratitude, but they never repay His loving compassion.

DAY 97

A Lifetime Award

O Lord, you alone are my hope.
I've trusted you, O LORD, from childhood.
PSALM 71:5 NLT

My heart swelled like an overinflated balloon. Tears blurred my vision as little Josh bounded for the stage, his blond cowlick flopping in the breeze. As his second grade Sunday school teacher, I had worked tirelessly to help him memorize ten Bible verses. Josh beamed at the shiny medal encircling his neck, but I knew that his true reward was God's Word implanted in his heart to guide him for the rest of his life.

DAY 98
Appreciation for Mercy

The LORD your God is a merciful God;
he will not abandon or destroy you.
DEUTERONOMY 4:31 NIV

Even when we fail God, He does not fail us. He knows our frailty and has mercy when we come to Him seeking forgiveness and wanting to change our ways. Mercy never holds grudges or seeks revenge, but it wants the best for forgiven sinners. So, our merciful Lord calls us to make changes that show we appreciate what He has done for us. Is some appreciation called for in your life?

DAY 99

Permission to Mourn

When I heard this, I sat down and cried.
Then for several days, I mourned; I went without
eating to show my sorrow, and I prayed.
NEHEMIAH 1:4 CEV

Bad news. When it arrives, what's your reaction? Do you scream? Fall apart? Run away? Nehemiah's response to bad news is a model for us. First, he vented his sorrow. It's okay to cry and mourn. Christians suffer pain like everyone else—only we know the source of inner healing. Disguising our struggle doesn't make us look more spiritual . . .just less real. Like Nehemiah, our next step is to turn to the only true source of help and comfort.

DAY 100
Joy in Our Troubles

Great is your love, reaching to the heavens;
your faithfulness reaches to the skies.
PSALM 57:10 NIV

Has God's mercy touched your life so deeply that you wanted to shout His praises to the skies? That's how the psalmist felt as he trusted in God, despite his troubles. When we look to God in our troubles, our burdened hearts can still find joy. Though we are small and weak, He is most powerful. His strength will overcome our deepest problems if only we let it.

DAY 101
Pebbles

"I will give you a new heart and put a new spirit within you; and I will remove the heart of stone from your flesh and give you a heart of flesh."

EZEKIEL 36:26 NASB

So many things can harden our hearts: overwhelming loss; shattered dreams; even scar tissue from broken hearts, disillusionment, and disappointment. To avoid pain, we simply turn off feelings. Our hearts become petrified rock—heavy, cold, and rigid. But God can crack our hearts of stone from the inside out and replace that miserable pile of pebbles with soft, feeling hearts of flesh. The amazing result is a brand-new, hope-filled spirit.

DAY 102
Overflowing Mercy

*Israel, put your hope in the LORD, for with
the LORD is unfailing love and with
him is full redemption.*

PSALM 130:7 NIV

Why hope in God, even in dire situations? Because every one of His people greatly needs His overflowing mercy. Our lives are frail, but He is not. Jesus brings the redemption we require. No matter what we face, Jesus walks with us. We need only trust faithfully that His salvation is on the way.

DAY 103
Do a Little Dance

*Then Miriam. . .took a tambourine and led
all the women as they played their
tambourines and danced.*
EXODUS 15:20 NLT

Can you imagine the enormous celebration that
broke out among the children of Israel when God
miraculously saved them from Pharaoh's army?
Even dignified prophetess Miriam grabbed her
tambourine and cut loose with her girlfriends.
Despite adverse circumstances, she heard God's
music and did His dance. Isn't that our goal
today? To Hear God's music above the world's
cacophony and do His dance as we recognize
everyday miracles in our lives?

DAY 104

Trust God

*Abraham answered, "God himself
will provide the lamb for the
burnt offering, my son."*
GENESIS 22:8 NIV

Though God had commanded Abraham to sacrifice his son Isaac, the patriarch had faith his son would not die. All it took was a ram caught in a bush. Because of Abraham's faith, the sheep was just where he needed it at the right moment. God provided just what was necessary—a sacrifice and a living son. Do you need God's provision today? Trust the God who made a way for Abraham to make a way for you too.

DAY 105
Payday

*"Go into all the world
and preach the gospel to all creation."*
MARK 16:15 NASB

One day as our family discussed the Great Commission over dinner, my salesman husband asked my young daughter if she knew what commission meant. "Sure," she replied. "It's what you get paid at the end for what you did in the beginning."

Our commission will be paid in heaven when we're surrounded not only by dear friends and family with whom we shared our faith, but also the souls reached by missions we supported with our time, money, and energies.

DAY 106

Let His Light Shine

For Christ's sake, I delight in weaknesses,
in insults, in hardships, in persecutions,
in difficulties. For when I am weak,
then I am strong.

2 Corinthians 12:10 niv

Only God can make you strong in the weak places. In those spots of persecution and hardship, His power and grace shine through your fragile vessel as you live as a faithful Christian. When you feel broken and useless, trust in Him to fill your flaws, and His light will shine through the cracks of your pain and reach a hurting world.

DAY 107
Soul Sister

"I always see the Lord near me, and I will not be afraid with him at my right side. Because of this, my heart will be glad, my words will be joyful, and I will live in hope."
ACTS 2:25–26 CEV

Laughter is the soul sister of joy; they often travel together. Humor is the primary catalyst for releasing joy into our souls and making our hearts glad. It's healthy for us too! Laughter is cleansing and healing, a powerful salve for the wounds of life. . .a natural medicine and tremendous stress reliever. Laughing is to joy what a 50 PERCENT OFF sign is to shopping. It motivates us to seek more, more, more!

DAY 108
Safe in His Will

Your hand will guide me,
your right hand will hold me fast.
PSALM 139:10 NIV

Need to make a life-changing decision? God wants to be part of it. As the psalmist understood, allowing Him to guide your steps means you won't get off track and land in a nasty situation. For the believer, the best place to be is in the palm of God's hand, safe from harm and in the center of His will.

DAY 109
JOY: Jesus Occupying You

May all who fear you find in me a cause for joy,
for I have put my hope in your word.
PSALM 119:74 NLT

Have you ever met someone you immediately knew was filled with joy? The kind of effervescent joy that bubbles up and overflows, covering everyone around her with warmth and love and acceptance. We love to be near people filled with Jesus-joy. And even more, as Christians, we want to be like them! Lord, remind us how.

DAY 110
Every Step of the Way

He will be our guide even to the end.
PSALM 48:14 NIV

When we are facing dire troubles, God never deserts us. As life ebbs away, He does not step back from our need. No, the Eternal One guides us every step of the way, whether life is joyous or discouraging. God never gives up on you and never fails you. So don't give up on yourself. When times are hard, grab onto Him more firmly. He will never leave you nor forsake you. And in the end, you will step into His arms in heaven.

As the Tide Turns

*"He will not falter or be discouraged till he
establishes justice on earth. In his teaching
the islands will put their hope."*
ISAIAH 42:4 NIV

Change. . .besides our unalterable Lord, it's the
only thing constant in this world. Yet the only
person who likes change is a baby with a wet
diaper. Isaiah prophesied that the Almighty
will one day create positive change on earth.
Like the tides that clean beach debris after a
storm, positive change washes away the old and
refreshes with the new. In this we hope.

DAY 112
You Can't Go Wrong

"In your unfailing love you will lead the people you have redeemed. In your strength you will guide them to your holy dwelling."
EXODUS 15:13 NIV

By following Jesus, you always head in the right direction. Though the way may seem dark or convoluted and you may often wonder if you're on the right track, as His Spirit leads you, you cannot go wrong. Your powerful Lord directs you in His everlasting way. If you start to go wrong, He will guide your steps. God's love never deserts His obedient child.

DAY 113

Up Is the Only Out

Let them lie face down in the dust,
for there may be hope at last.

LAMENTATIONS 3:29 NLT

The Old Testament custom for grieving people was to lie prostrate and cover themselves with ashes. Perhaps the thought was that when you're wallowing in the dust, at least you can't descend any further. There's an element of hope in knowing that there's only one way to go: up. If a recent loss has you sprawled in the dust, know that God doesn't waste pain in our lives. He will use it for some redeeming purpose.

DAY 114
Unfailing Love

*The LORD delights in those who. . .
put their hope in his unfailing love.*
PSALM 147:11 NIV

We can hope in a lot of things that fail us miserably, or we can enjoy a blind optimism that leads us into trouble. But when we hope in God, who has loved us completely, our faith cannot fail. Could the One who delights in our trust forget to bless our anticipation of an eternity with Him?

Make God joyful today as you put your trust in His everlasting love.

Welcome Back

*Train up a child in the way he should go:
and when he is old, he will not depart from it.*
PROVERBS 22:6 KJV

I'll never forget the tender bedtime family gatherings on my sister's bed when I was a child. After reading a Bible story from the big picture Bible, we took turns praying. When I had children, I established the same tradition in our home. The Bible promises that if we instill God's Word and principles in our children, they will one day return to it. It may take time, but God's Word will not return void.

DAY 116
Prosperity Returns

*"Then I will make up to you for the years
that the swarming locust has eaten."*
JOEL 2:25 NASB

Those of us who rejoice in God can trust that even though the consuming locusts of life destroy our blessings, God will replace them. Though hardship makes us struggle awhile, God turns the situation around and pours out blessings on His faithful people. Prosperity returns to those who love Him well. In heaven or on earth, the blessing appears again.

DAY 117

Time Out for Encouragement

*"Do all that is in your heart,
for the LORD is with you."*
2 SAMUEL 7:3 NKJV

Every day, why not encourage yourself? Take a few moments to fill your thoughts with gentle words of assurance and affirmation. Reflect on God's many kindnesses toward you in the past, and visualize the good plans He has for you right now. If you're lacking energy or feeling unappreciated, let Him whisper words of assurance in your heart. No, it's not just a trick to get yourself pumped for the duties of the day, but the way God renews a tired spirit, boosts sagging confidence, heightens appreciation for the present hour, and restores genuine enthusiasm.

DAY 118

Praise God—
No Matter What

The king will rejoice in God;
all who swear by God will glory in him.
PSALM 63:11 NIV

Need some joy in your life? Start praising God, and no matter what messy situations you face today, you'll begin rejoicing. Praise Him for who He is—His immense, loving nature that has blessed you so much. Thank Him for the love He's showered on you. As you remember His love, sorrow loses its grasp on your life.

DAY 119

Rocky Road

For through the Spirit we eagerly await by faith
the righteousness for which we hope.
GALATIANS 5:5 NIV

My daughter's five-pound Russian Terror (oops—that's Terrier) is anything but righteous. Rocky dashes after cars, nibbles poisonous plants, and routinely ingests ripped-apart rugs. In order to guide said pup along the path of righteousness, doors must close. Our paths of righteousness are also guided by the One who shuts doors according to what's best for us. So, girlfriends—enough howling, whining, and scratching at closed doors!

DAY 120
God Is Great

I know that the LORD is great,
that our Lord is greater than all gods.
PSALM 135:5 NIV

Other "gods" contend with Jesus in the marketplace of ideas, and devout Christians may encounter contention. But just as the psalmist recognized God's greatness, we can too as we look at the world around us. No other would-be deity shows forth its glory in creation. No other has provided God's gracious salvation. If our Lord controls our lives, how can we look to any other gods?

DAY 121
Not Suzie Homemaker

*The Spirit has given each of us
a special way of serving others.*
1 Corinthians 12:7 cev

My friend Denise has the gift of hospitality. She welcomes people into her home and makes them feel loved through her thoughtful accents: serving food on her best china, lighting scented candles, offering cozy furnishings. Hospitality is not my gift. My guests get bagged chips, flat soda, and leave coated in cat hair. God taught me not to compare and despair, for He has given each of us our own gift to be used for His service. What's yours?

DAY 122
Live Devotedly

*Do you not know that you are the temple of God
and that the Spirit of God dwells in you?*
1 CORINTHIANS 3:16 NKJV

God lives within you, not in a distant place. When you act according to His Word, He acts. When you fail, people may begin to doubt Him. That's why Paul encourages you to live devotedly for your Lord. As one of His people, you're filled with His potent Spirit, who empowers you to live a holy life. Live in His strength always.

DAY 123
Working Out

I will never give up hope or stop praising you.
PSALM 71:14 CEV

Praise is like a muscle: if we don't exercise it regularly, it becomes weak and atrophied. But if we flex and extend an attitude of gratitude daily, praise grows into a strong, dependable force that nurtures hope and carries us through the worst of circumstances. Like Helen Keller, though blind and deaf, we'll praise our Creator: "I thank God for my handicaps, for through them, I have found myself, my work, and my God."

DAY 124
Love Is Action

*Dear friends, let us love one another, for love
comes from God. Everyone who loves has
been born of God and knows God.*

1 JOHN 4:7 NIV

Want to see love? Look at God. Seeking love in
this world is bound to be confusing. But in our
Lord, we see the clean, clear lines of real love—
love we can share with our families, friends, and
fellow believers. Love for our enemies. Love for
our Savior. Apart from God, we cannot truly and
sacrificially love others. Love isn't just a feeling,
but the actions we take as we follow Him.

DAY 125
Inexplicable Strength

"The joy of the LORD is your strength."
Nehemiah 8:10 nasb

Joy is not based on the circumstances around us. It is not synonymous with happiness. God promised believers His deep, abiding joy—not fleeting happiness, which is here today, gone tomorrow. The joy of the Lord rises above external situations and supernaturally overshadows everything else to become our inexplicable, internal strength.

DAY 126
Seeing God

No one has seen God at any time.
If we love one another, God abides in us,
and His love has been perfected in us.

1 JOHN 4:12 NKJV

How do we see God? Often, it's through other people. That's why it's important to have a compassionate Christian witness—people see you and think God is like you if you claim His name. In that way, many people have gotten erroneous concepts about the Savior. But many more have come to love Him through faithful testimonies. Today you can love others and show them clearly what Jesus looks like.

DAY 127
Forever Joy

We don't look at the troubles we can see now. . . .
For the things we see now will soon be gone,
but the things we cannot see will last forever.
2 CORINTHIANS 4:18 NLT

A painter's first brush strokes look like random blobs—no discernable shape, substance, or clue as to what the completed painting will be. But in time, the skilled artist brings order to perceived chaos. Initial confusion is forgotten in joyful admiration of the finished masterpiece.

We often can't see past the blobs of trouble on our life canvases. We must trust that the Artist has a masterpiece underway. And there will be great joy in its completion.

DAY 128
Life-Altering Impact

We were therefore buried with him through baptism into death in order that, just as Christ was raised from the dead through the glory of the Father, we too may live a new life.

ROMANS 6:4 NIV

Baptism is a picture of the old, sinful nature's death and the new faith life God gives those who trust in Him. Belief in Jesus has a life-altering impact. One moment a sinful person is dead, held in sin's grasp. The next she becomes an entirely new person, alive in her Savior. Only Jesus offers this glorious freedom. Has He given it to you?

DAY 129
Perfect Love

Love never gives up, never loses faith,
is always hopeful, and endures
through every circumstance.

1 Corinthians 13:7 nlt

We have relationships in three directions: upward (with God), outward (with others), and inward (with ourselves). We are bound to be disappointed at one time or another by the latter two. Because of human frailty, we will inevitably experience failure by others and even ourselves. Our imperfect love will be strained to the breaking point. But our Creator will never fail us—His perfect love never gives up on us.

DAY 130

Living in the Light

In him was life,
and that life was the light of all mankind.
JOHN 1:4 NIV

Jesus is a Christian's life and light, as anyone who has walked with Him for a while can tell you. Everything is different once He enters a soul. As a result, the new believer begins to make changes, cleaning out the dark corners of her existence so that the bright light shining within her will not fall on dirty places. She's living in the light, following Jesus.

DAY 131
Three Little Words

*Three things will last
forever—faith, hope, and love.*
1 CORINTHIANS 13:13 NLT

Don't you get tired of throwing away panty hose? It's hard to believe that modern technology can scan quivers inside our livers and detect nickel-sized puddles on Mars, but we still can't manufacture hose that won't run. Yep, there are precious few things that endure. Only three, the Bible says: faith, hope, and love. Three things that will never break down, wear out, or get lost. These are the only things worth keeping.

DAY 132
You Are Valuable

Who can find a virtuous woman?
for her price is far above rubies.
PROVERBS 31:10 KJV

Are you a virtuous woman? If so, you are truly valuable, no matter how unbelievers criticize you. Proverbs 31 says you can have a profitable life with good relationships, a happy home life, and successful business ventures if you run your life according to God's principles. So don't worry about the opinions of others if they don't mesh with God's. Instead, obey Him and be a valuable jewel to your Lord.

DAY 133
New Life

*God is so good, and by raising Jesus
from death, he has given us new life
and a hope that lives on.*
1 PETER 1:3 CEV

The words of a song I wrote while pregnant with my first child exult in the similarities between new physical life and fresh spiritual life in Christ: "New life stirs within me now. Like a soft breeze, transforming me now. It's a miracle of love, precious blessing from above. My heart has taken wings. . .lift me up!"

New life. By the goodness of God, we can experience this precious transformation no less miraculous than a baby growing within us.

DAY 134
Love and Obey

"Whoever has my commands and keeps
them is the one who loves me."
JOHN 14:21 NIV

Do you feel you love God with all your heart?
Then show it by obeying Him. Jesus paved the
path for you. Through His own sacrificial life, He
showed you what it means to obey the Father. A
Christian who lives for herself rather than God
shows wavering commitment. One who loves God
wholeheartedly walks in Jesus' way, obeying His
commands in scripture. Here is where we start:
Love God? Then obey Him too.

DAY 135
Time-out

"The LORD will not abandon His people."
1 SAMUEL 12:22 NASB

Do you remember when, as a little girl, you languished alone in your room as punishment? Or maybe you sat with your nose plastered to the corner in time-out. It felt like your parents had abandoned you, didn't it? As adults, we sometimes feel abandoned when that's not the case at all. We're actually in a place strategically chosen by a loving Father to teach us, broaden us, and improve us in the end.

DAY 136
Blessings Will Come

"All these blessings shall come upon you
and overtake you, because you obey
the voice of the LORD your God."

DEUTERONOMY 28:2 NKJV

Obey God; receive blessings. It seems simple enough, doesn't it? Then why do we obey and only get in more trouble than before? Perhaps it's because we're looking at it from our perspective, not His. Blessings do not always follow on the heels of obedience; they often take time to appear. Today's blessings may result from long-ago faithfulness. But because God has promised, we know good things come if only we wait.

DAY 137
Bigger and Better

*Waiting does not diminish us, any more
than waiting diminishes a pregnant
mother. . . . The longer we wait. . .
the more joyful our expectancy.*
ROMANS 8:24–25 MSG

Life is filled with waiting—on slow people, transportation, doctor reports, even for God to act. Waiting often requires patience we don't have. It feels like perpetual pregnancy—anticipating a baby that is never delivered. The secret is to clasp hands with our Lord. He offers His shield of protection from impatience, irritability, and anger and replaces them with self-control, kindness, and joy. Waiting is inevitable, but we can draw closer to the Father in the waiting.

DAY 138
Into Eternity

Blessed are they that do his commandments,
that they may have right to the tree of life,
and may enter in through the gates into the city.
REVELATION 22:14 KJV

The blessings of obedience not only impact us today, they follow us into eternity. Whatever we do to please God never dies. By trusting in Jesus, the works that demonstrate our faith give us joy now and remain secure for the future in the One who never changes. We look forward to life in the New Jerusalem even as we reap His blessings now.

DAY 139

Please Rescue Me

I long for you to rescue me!
Your word is my only hope.
PSALM 119:81 CEV

Have you ever longed to be rescued?

Stranded after shredding knee ligaments during a remote mountain skiing accident, I waited helplessly for rescuers to arrive. All alone on the raw Canadian mountainside, I felt fear mount. Freezing temperatures, prowling cougars, and unrelenting pain threatened to engulf me in despair. So I did the most and the least I could do: I prayed and recited scripture. And my faithful heavenly Father rescued me with His peace.

DAY 140
God Hears

"Therefore I tell you, whatever you ask for in prayer, believe that you have received it, and it will be yours."

MARK 11:24 NIV

This verse is not prescribing some magical incantation, but faith that God hears and answers our requests. When we trust that He knows our needs and wants to respond to them, we are in a position to receive. Would Jesus be proud of our requests? Do we seek the good of others? Or do we look only to our own desires? God answers prayers that reflect His will. How do yours stack up against this measure?

DAY 141
Hope Resurrected

We had hoped that he would be the one to set Israel free! But it has already been three days since all this happened.

LUKE 24:21 CEV

The scenario for this scripture is quite unusual. Two of Jesus' disciples are describing their lost hope due to the events surrounding Jesus' death to none other than Jesus Himself. They don't recognize Him as they walk together on the road to Emmaus after His resurrection. Spiritual cataracts blind them to the hope they thought was dead—right in front of them! Let's open our spiritual eyes to Jesus, who is walking beside us.

DAY 142

Love Your Enemy

*"But I tell you, love your enemies
and pray for those who persecute you."*
MATTHEW 5:44 NIV

Without God's strength, could any of us follow this command of Jesus for more than a very brief time? Consistently loving an enemy is a real challenge. If you hurt from pain inflicted by another, you hardly want to pray for her. But loving actions and prayer can bring great peace between two people at odds with each other. For those who consistently follow this command, strife may not last forever.

DAY 143
Sprung

I will free your prisoners from death in a waterless
dungeon. Come back to the place of safety,
all you prisoners who still have hope!
ZECHARIAH 9:11–12 NLT

In the marvelous book *The Count of Monte Cristo*, Edmond Dantes is unjustly imprisoned. Against all odds, God enables him to escape and eventually return victorious, a hope-filled man.

Have you ever felt trapped in a prison of hopelessness? Financial difficulties, poor health, unemployment, rocky marriage, delinquent children—there are countless dungeons that shackle us. But God promises hope and freedom from our prisons. Jesus bailed us out!

DAY 144

Healing Power

The prayer of faith will save the sick,
and the Lord will raise him up. And if he
has committed sins, he will be forgiven.

JAMES 5:15 NKJV

Have you seen the amazing healing power of prayer? As faithful Christians lift a sufferer up to God, He works in the body but also in the heart and soul. Know someone who is ill? Pray for physical health to return. But don't forget to include spiritual needs, for the Great Physician treats the whole person. Some spiritual issue may be the real problem that requires healing.

DAY 145
Power Source

*He gives strength to the weary
and increases the power of the weak.*
ISAIAH 40:29 NIV

Sometimes we feel as if our backs will break under the burdens we carry: debt, responsibilities, impossible schedules. But our God promises to strengthen and empower us if we turn to Him for help. He knows. He cares. He is able.

It's been written that persecuted European Christians don't pray for God to lessen their loads like American Christians do. Instead, they pray for stronger backs.

DAY 146
Prayer from the Heart

Some trust in chariots, and some in horses; but we will remember the name of the LORD our God.

PSALM 20:7 NKJV

This may seem an odd prayer for a king going out to battle, but it shows where David's heart was. He knew his war equipment could fail, but God could not.

What danger can we face that God is incapable of defending us from? None. Where have we placed our trust—in Him or in worldly defenses?

DAY 147
No Call-Waiting

*"Call on me and come and pray to me,
and I will listen to you."*
JEREMIAH 29:12 NIV

"I will listen to you." Every woman's dream.

Jeremiah knew the importance of being listened to. He proclaimed God's message for forty years to the unseeing, unhearing, unresponsive nation of Judah. His ironic good news: God is listening!

Do you ever feel like no one's listening? The Bible says God hears us every time we utter His name. How precious we are to our Creator that He bends His omnipotent ear each time we call on Him.

DAY 148
Overcoming the Sin Barrier

Godly sorrow brings repentance that leads
to salvation and leaves no regret.
2 CORINTHIANS 7:10 NIV

Godly sorrow comes when we feel the pain of our own sins. As we recognize our own wrongdoing and know that our actions have hurt us, others, and even the heart of God, we reach the place to do something about it. We repent, and God offers His salvation.

Has sin come between you and your Savior? Turn at once in sorrow and ask Him to make everything right in your heart and soul. You'll never be sorry you did.

DAY 149
Juiced

God is our refuge and strength,
a very present help in trouble.
PSALM 46:1 NASB

Remember the scene from the movie *Air Force One*, when Harrison Ford, as the U.S. president, calls for help from the belly of a terrorist-hijacked plane after much death-defying effort? Just as the crucial call is dialed, his cell phone battery conks out. Can you identify? What a relief that our direct line to God—prayer—is always juiced and never needs recharging!

DAY 150
Cleansing Spirit

I came not to call the righteous,
but sinners to repentance.
LUKE 5:32 KJV

Repentance isn't meant for "good people" who have only "tiny" sins to confess. This verse reminds us that no sin is too awful for God to hear about it. God calls all who are sinful—those who most need Him and have the most to fear from His awesome holiness. Each of us may hesitate to confess sins and admit to wrongs that embarrass us. But we are just the ones He calls. One moment of repentance and His Spirit cleanses our lives.

DAY 151
Slip-Sliding Away

Instruct those who are rich. . .not to be conceited or to fix their hope on the uncertainty of riches, but on God, who richly supplies us with all things to enjoy.
1 TIMOTHY 6:17 NASB

My friend Claire lived large with a millionaire husband, enormous house, designer clothes, and flashy convertible—even a cook (to my envy!). But suddenly the economy headed south, and in the twinkle of a bank vault key, she lost it all. Divorced, homeless, and bitter, Claire was forced to wait tables to pay her ill son's medical bills. We can't depend on money—here today, gone tomorrow. Our hope must be fixed on our eternal God.

DAY 152

Compassion to Others

*"And if he sins against you seven times in
a day, and seven times in a day returns to you,
saying, 'I repent,' you shall forgive him."*

LUKE 17:4 NKJV

When another offends us, do we pass on the
forgiveness we have received? That's what Jesus
commanded. Remembering how gracious God
has been to us, we need to show it to those who
affront us too. As we think of our many sins that
God put behind His back, can we fail to show
compassion to others?

DAY 153
Daily Duties

Let all that you do be done in love.
1 CORINTHIANS 16:14 NASB

Sometimes we get so wrapped up in our daily to-do lists that we put our duties above people. "Leave me alone until this project is finished, kids." "Sorry, Sue, I'm too busy to have lunch." "Oh, I don't have time to talk to Mom today; I'll let the answering machine get it."

How, then, can we ever share the love of Christ with those we've shoved out of our way? People don't care how much you know until they know how much you care.

DAY 154
Available 24-7

*"Blessed is the man to whom
the Lord shall not impute sin."*
Romans 4:8 nkjv

Sin forgiven: what a wonderful thought! No longer do we need to be dragged into wrongdoing, because God has cleansed our hearts. His Spirit sweeps through us, lifting the burden of sin from our lives. Though we still fail, in Christ, God will not hold the sin against us. Forgiveness, available 24-7, sends His Spirit through our lives again and again.

DAY 155
One Nation under God

*The poor are filled with hope,
and injustice is silenced.*
JOB 5:16 CEV

"Give me your tired, your poor, your huddled masses..." beckons the Statue of Liberty, offering a home and freedom to hurting people. Many of our ancestors flocked to American shores that were offering freedom of worship and an end to the injustice of religious persecution. May we never forget the sacrifices they made to pursue the hope of providing their children—you and me—with a nation founded on Christian principles. Let's strive to preserve that hope for future generations.

DAY 156
Reconcilers

God was reconciling the world to himself in Christ, not counting people's sins against them. And he has committed to us the message of reconciliation.

2 CORINTHIANS 5:19 NIV

The Lord loved you so much that He paid a huge price to draw you into His arms. Jesus' sacrifice destroyed the sin barrier that separates humanity and God. Those who repent are reconciled to their holy God. But faith does not stop there. He makes us reconcilers too as He sends us out with the message that has meant so much: "God loves you too."

DAY 157
A Strong Tower

The name of the LORD is a fortified tower;
the righteous run to it and are safe.

PROVERBS 18:10 NIV

We of the twenty-first century tend to limit our references to God, but ancient Hebrew translations offer a broader perspective. There is intrinsic hope in the names of God: Elohim (Mighty Creator), El Olam (The Everlasting God), Yahweh Yireh (The Lord Will Provide), Yahweh Shalom (The Lord Is Peace), Yahweh Tsuri (The Lord, My Rock), and Abba (Father) to name a few. Let's broaden our scope of His powerful name in our prayers today.

DAY 158
Saving Grace

My soul finds rest in God;
my salvation comes from him.
PSALM 62:1 NIV

At the moment you repented of your sins and asked Jesus to control your life, God saved you. But He didn't stop there. Each day of your life, He continues His saving work. He redirects you, protects you, and provides for your every need. In any trouble, rest in Him. He will not fail.

DAY 159

24-7

He will not let your foot slip—he who watches over you will not slumber.

PSALM 121:3 NIV

I love hiking the winding mountain paths near our remote Smoky Mountain cabin. Sometimes I get so caught up in watching hummingbirds or admiring cliff-side vistas that I stumble, forgetting that inattention could be deadly. How comforting to know that our Lord is always alert as He watches over us. We don't have to worry that an important prayer will slip by while He sneezes or that He'll nap through our surgery. He's always on duty.

DAY 160
Shine for Him

[Jesus] gave himself for us to redeem us
from all wickedness and to purify for
himself a people that are his very own,
eager to do what is good.

TITUS 2:14 NIV

Is there any sin from which Jesus cannot save us? No. As long as we look to Him, He will lead us into increasing, joyous holiness.

God takes sinful people and changes their lives, making them His hands in an evil world. As His people draw near Him, putting off sin, their good works shine forth the nature of their Savior. Will you shine for Him today?

DAY 161
One Gutsy Gal

"It could be that you were made queen for a time like this!"
ESTHER 4:14 CEV

Crowned queen after winning a beauty contest, Esther was only allowed audience with her king when summoned. A wave of his scepter would pardon her from execution, but he was a hard man—and unpredictable. When Esther learned of a plot to destroy her people, she faced a tough decision. She was the only one who could save them—at supreme risk. God had intentionally placed her in that position for that time. What's your divinely ordained position?

DAY 162
Our Partner

Continue to work out your salvation
with fear and trembling.
PHILIPPIANS 2:12 NIV

Salvation is hard work! Not only did it require Jesus' crucifixion for our sins, but we have a part in the effort too. We have to live out the commands in God's Word that make our faith have an impact on our world. But we need not feel discouraged, for we are not alone in the labor. God acts through us, by His Spirit. What better working partner could we have than God Himself?

DAY 163
Cool Summer Shower

He will renew your life
and sustain you in your old age.
RUTH 4:15 NIV

Ruth's blessing of renewal is applicable to us today. *Renovatio* is Latin for "rebirth." It means casting off the old and embracing the new: a revival of spirit, a renovation of attitude. Something essential for women to espouse every day of their lives. Like a cool rain shower on a sizzling summer day, Ruth's hope was renewed by her Lord's touch, and ours will be too if we look to Him for daily replenishing.

DAY 164
Spiritual Training

All Scripture. . .is useful for. . .training in righteousness, so that the servant of God may be thoroughly equipped for every good work.
2 TIMOTHY 3:16–17 NIV

Did you realize that God prepares you to do good works every day of your life? Because you believe in Him, He will lead you to do good, following His plan for your life.

How do you start? By reading the scriptures, His guidebook. There you will learn what to believe, how to act, and how to speak with love. Soon you'll be ready to put into action all you've learned.

DAY 165
Zombie Zone

Be joyful in hope,
patient in affliction, faithful in prayer.
ROMANS 12:12 NIV

Affliction has a tendency to suck the joy right out of our lives, leaving us stranded in the dully-funks. You know—that black hole of existence where our minds fog, emotions go numb, eyes glaze over, and we languish in a state of spiritual dullness. A spiritual zombie zone. But if we're faithful in prayer, God will be faithful to rescue us from those joy-sucking dully-funks and fill us to the brim with His abundant joy.

DAY 166
Serving Others

*You. . .were called to be free. But do not use
your freedom to indulge the flesh; rather,
serve one another humbly in love.*
GALATIANS 5:13 NIV

As women, we know a lot about serving: we serve
on many fronts and sometimes wonder why this
is our lot. God tells us He freed us from sin, not
to do what we like but so we can share His love.
If we're tempted to fulfill our own sinful desires,
let's remind ourselves why we are here—we obey
Jesus by doing good for others. If that's not our
goal, we need redirection from Him.

DAY 167
Laughter and Hope

A joyful heart is good medicine.
PROVERBS 17:22 NASB

Laughter is to hope as nonstick cooking spray is to a shiny new muffin tin: it keeps the goo from sticking. Once the batter of everyday responsibility hardens and adheres to our attitudes, it's awfully hard to scrape off enough crust for hope to shine through. But if we coat our day with a little laughter and the joy of the Lord, problems will slide off a lot better. And hope sparkles.

DAY 168
You're Equipped

In Christ you have been brought to fullness.
He is the head over every power and authority.
COLOSSIANS 2:10 NIV

Do you feel incomplete or inadequate, unable to carry out the tasks God has given you? You aren't, you know, if you tap into His Spirit. God equips you to do all things in Him. If you feel overwhelmed, make sure you haven't taken on tasks rightfully belonging to someone else. God does not overload your life with busyness. He has a purpose for all you do. So be certain you're serving in the right place, doing the work He planned for you.

DAY 169
Two-Stranded Rope

*The widow who is really in need and left
all alone puts her hope in God and
continues night and day to pray
and to ask God for help.*

1 TIMOTHY 5:5 NIV

Some women feel as though they are irreparably weakened when they are widowed. Where there once were three strands of a sturdy rope (his, hers, and God's), there now are two. But those who persevere through faith and true grit say the secret is to learn to rejoice in what's left instead of lamenting what has been lost. Look forward. Move forward. Keep that two-stranded rope strong, and never lose hope of a better tomorrow.

DAY 170
Grace Is a Gift

But unto every one of us is given grace according to the measure of the gift of Christ.
EPHESIANS 4:7 KJV

We don't usually think of grace as a "spiritual gift." But consider: it's the basis for all the gifts God gives us. Without His gracious forgiveness, we'd have nothing spiritually. Our sins so separate us, that only His forgiveness allows us to approach Him. Whether we receive a large measure of grace or a smaller one, it is the perfect gift, given by Jesus, just for us. Let's appreciate what it cost Him and walk in Him today.

DAY 171
Bet the Farm

*Whoever plows and threshes should be able to
do so in the hope of sharing in the harvest.*
1 CORINTHIANS 9:10 NIV

There's a young man who works in children's
church with me who is loud, brash, impulsive,
an incessant talker, and loves the Lord with all
his heart. The kids think he's hilarious. I think
he's obnoxious. But I must remind myself that
God uses him in unique ways to reach young
hearts with the Gospel that I never could. He's
a plowman and I'm a thresher, and we work
together to harvest souls into God's kingdom.

DAY 172

For His Glory

We have different gifts,
according to the grace given to each of us.
ROMANS 12:6 NIV

Your spiritual gifts are tailored especially for you. God has a purpose for your life. To help you accomplish it, He has given just the gifts you need—nothing more, nothing less. Doesn't knowing that God has gifted you in just the right way make you feel special? Thank Him for those gifts today, and use them for the glory of His kingdom and to help others.

The Salvage Master

We are pressed on every side by troubles,
but we are not crushed.

2 Corinthians 4:8 nlt

Many women struggle with depression at some point in their lives: postpartum, kids-partum (empty nest), brain-partum (menopause), and anytime in between. We feel that we are being compressed into a rock-hard cube like the product of a trash compactor. The normal details of life suddenly become perplexing and overwhelming. But God does not abandon us to the garbage dump. He is the Salvage Master and recycles us into sterling images of His glory.

DAY 174
Reach Out

*Try to excel in [gifts] that
build up the church.*
1 Corinthians 14:12 niv

Paul's words to the Corinthians were meant for us too. We should build up the church, not ourselves, through our spiritual gifts. When God gave you a special combination of spiritual abilities, it wasn't to make you feel important. He designed them to help you reach out to those who need to accept Him as Savior and to support believers who also have your mission to reach the world. Is that how you're using your gifts today?

DAY 175
Look to the Sunrise

I rise before dawn and cry for help;
I have put my hope in your word.
PSALM 119:147 NIV

Could be stress or worry or berserk hormones. Whatever the cause, many women find themselves staring at their dark bedroom ceilings in the wee morning hours. We try counting sheep, but they morph into naughty little children, and we exhaust ourselves chasing them through fitful dreams. We're tormented by the "what ifs," guilted by the "should haves," and jolted wider awake by the "don't forget tos." But a new day is dawning, and help is but a prayer away.

DAY 176
Christian Strength

*Finally, be strong in the Lord
and in his mighty power.*
EPHESIANS 6:10 NIV

When you rely on God's strength, what are you tapping into? Not some small pool of power that fails at a critical moment. The Christian's strength is mighty because God is mighty. He who created the universe does not have a short arm that cannot reach down to your situation. Shining stars testify to His authority. Galaxies in space are ordered by His hand. He can order your life too. Ask Him to use His strength in your life, and you will have all you need.

DAY 177
Chill

*I lie awake thinking of you, meditating on you
through the night. Because you are my helper,
I sing for joy in the shadow of your wings.*

PSALM 63:6–7 NLT

Are you a worrier? Do you frequently find
yourself working up a sweat building molehills
into mountains during the midnight hours? This
passage suggests an alternative for that nasty
and unproductive habit. Instead of worrying, try
meditating on the loving-kindness of God. Like a
distressed chick tucked safely beneath the snug
wings of the mother hen, allow the joy of being
loved and protected to relax your tense muscles
and ease you into peaceful rest.

DAY 178
Have Courage

Be on your guard; stand firm in the faith;
be courageous; be strong.
1 CORINTHIANS 16:13 NIV

Being a Christian can take lots of courage. As the world around us becomes increasingly hostile to God and our personal lives become tense because of our beliefs, we feel the challenge. But we are not defenseless. Christians through the ages have faced these troubles and triumphed. The Lord who supported them gives us strength too. Let us stand fast for Jesus, calling on His Spirit to strengthen our lives. Then we will be strong indeed.

DAY 179
Showers of Blessing

Do the skies themselves send down showers?
No, it is you, LORD our God. Therefore our hope is
in you, for you are the one who does all this.
JEREMIAH 14:22 NIV

Have you ever stood in your parched garden, praying for rain? The plants you've nurtured from seeds are wilting, flower petals litter the ground, fruit withers on the vine. Then thunder clouds roll, and the skies burst forth with reinvigorating rain.

There will be dry times too in our spiritual gardens, but our hope is in the Lord our God, who sends showers to revive us. Deluge us today, Lord.

DAY 180
Uplift Others

We who are strong ought to bear with the failings of the weak and not to please ourselves.

ROMANS 15:1 NIV

So God has made you strong in some area—perhaps by experience, as you have struggled to obey Him. Now, how do you respond to others? Don't criticize those who have different experiences or other strengths, or carp about the failings of new, weak Christians. Instead, use your power to uplift others. Come alongside and help. Then God's strength will have helped you both.

DAY 181
Snippets of Hope

I also pray that you will understand the incredible greatness of God's power for us who believe him.
EPHESIANS 1:19 NLT

Daydreams are snippets of hope for our souls. Yearnings for something better, something more exciting, something that lifts our spirits. Some dreams are mere fancy, but others are meant to last a lifetime because God embedded them in our hearts. It's when we lose sight of those dreams that hope dies.

But God offers us access to His almighty power—the very same greatness that brought His Son back from the dead. What greater hope is there?

DAY 182
Make the Most

*Since everything will be destroyed in this
way, what kind of people ought you to be?
You ought to live holy and godly lives.*

2 PETER 3:11 NIV

Knowing that the world will not last forever,
how should we act? We have no devil-may-care
option, in which we act as if eternity does not
matter, because God calls us to live wholly for
Him. The world's destruction should not make
us careless, but vigilant to make the most of our
time. In the end, all we do here will not be lost
but will pass on into eternity.

DAY 183
True Success

"For I know the plans I have for you," declares the
LORD, *"plans to prosper you. . .plans to*
give you hope and a future."
JEREMIAH 29:11 NIV

As little girls, we dream about the handsome man we'll one day marry, exciting trips we'll take, the mansion we'll call home, and the beautiful, perfect children we'll have. A successful life—isn't that what we hope for?

But God doesn't call us to be successful; He calls us to trust Him. We may never be successful in the world's eyes, but trust in our Father's omnipotence ensures our future and our hope. And that's true success.

DAY 184
You Have Gifts!

Now to each one the manifestation of the Spirit is given for the common good.
1 CORINTHIANS 12:7 NIV

Did you know that you are a gifted person? God gives each of His children spiritual gifts designed to help themselves and others—wisdom, knowledge, faith, healing, to name just a few. As you grow spiritually, you begin to unwrap those presents from God. Over time, you may be surprised and feel blessed at how many He's provided for you.

Feeling unimportant? Remind yourself that you're gifted by God!

DAY 185
I Can't Lose!

Alive, I'm Christ's messenger; dead, I'm his prize.
Life versus even more life! I can't lose.
PHILIPPIANS 1:21 MSG

The old-timer smiled at his granddaughter as she rebuked him for driving the farm tractor. "Don't you know the danger at your age, Grandpa? You could be killed!"

"I'm not worried, darlin', and you shouldn't be either. What's the worst that could happen? I wake up in heaven. This life versus an even better one. . .for all eternity."

When worry begins to overshadow hope, remember three little words from Philippians: I can't lose!

DAY 186
Eternal Blessings

A faithful man will abound with blessings, but he who hastens to be rich will not go unpunished.
PROVERBS 28:20 NKJV

Faithfulness to God or success in the world: Have you had to choose between them? Seeking the world's goals brings short-term benefits, but only God provides abundant and ongoing blessings for those who put serving Him first in their lives. Though worldly blessings last for a day, a year, or a few years, they cannot remain for eternity. When you consider success, think of the kind that really lasts.

DAY 187
Easy as ABC

God has done all this, so that we will look
for him and reach out and find him.
He isn't far from any of us.

ACTS 17:27 CEV

God is near. But we must reach out for Him. There's a line that we choose to cross, a specific action we take. We can't ooze into the kingdom of God; it's an intentional decision. It's simple, really—as simple as ABC. A is Admitting we're sinful and in need of a Savior. B is Believing that Jesus died for our sins and rose from the grave. C is Committing our lives to Him. Life everlasting is then ours.

DAY 188
Living in Him

The meek will inherit the land
and enjoy peace and prosperity.
PSALM 37:11 NIV

You might call this God's definition of success: a profitable land that provides for His people and His peace that provides a blessed life. Notice that money and other possessions aren't mentioned. But the peace of living in Him flows freely to those who abide in Him. Would this be success to you? If not, what does it tell you about your spiritual life?

DAY 189
Bestseller

The mystery is that Christ lives in you,
and he is your hope of sharing in God's glory.
COLOSSIANS 1:27 CEV

Everybody loves a good mystery—as long as the plot twists a bit and the good guy wins in the end. The Christian life is a mystery. It's baffling that God could love us so deeply that He sent His only Son to suffer and die for us. And now the risen Christ lives in our hearts, bridging the gap between us and God forever. What an incredible page-turner!

DAY 190
Ask Jesus

Because he himself suffered when he was tempted,
he is able to help those who are being tempted.
HEBREWS 2:18 NIV

Why can Jesus help us when temptation strikes? Because He's walked a mile in our shoes. He knows how strongly sin attracts us. But because He never fell prey to it, He can effectively show us how to resist even the strongest enticement. The biggest mistakes we make are not calling on Him and not persistently seeking His powerful aid when Satan repeatedly lures us into sin. Need help? Just ask Jesus.

DAY 191
Survivor

The terrible storm raged for many days. . .until at last all hope was gone.
ACTS 27:20 NLT

Following a lovely renewal of our wedding vows on our tenth anniversary, my husband and I boarded a Caribbean cruise ship. Tragically, Hurricane Gilbert obliterated our destination, Cancun, before hurling our ship back and forth on twelve-foot waves for four interminable days. I felt hopeless, sick as a pup, and at the mercy of the storm. Life's like that, isn't it? Unexpected storms blow up, blot out the light, and toss us about. But we are survivors!

DAY 192
God's Protection

The Lord knows how to deliver the godly out of temptations and to reserve the unjust under punishment for the day of judgment.

2 PETER 2:9 NKJV

Feeling surrounded by temptations? God hasn't forgotten you. He knows how to protect His children from harm and offers His wisdom to His children. Maybe you need to avoid places that could lead you into sin—that may mean taking action like finding a new job or new friends. When God is trying to protect you, don't resist. Sin is never better than knowing Him.

Prune Juice, Anyone?

*Therefore, with minds that are alert and fully
sober, set your hope on the grace to be brought to
you when Jesus Christ is revealed.*

1 PETER 1:13 NIV

Diets are the devil. They exclude chocolate éclairs and hinge on effective use of that dreaded *s* word: self-control. In the fruit bowl of the Spirit, self-control is the prune. It's hard to swallow but nonetheless essential to our faith—especially where hope is concerned. If self-control isn't exercised, we can find our spirits soaring up and down faster than the numbers on our bathroom scales. Like prunes, daily use of self-control regulates us and prepares us for action.

DAY 194
Give Thanks

Give thanks to the God of gods.
His love endures forever.
PSALM 136:2 NIV

Having trouble being thankful? Read Psalm 136. You'll be reminded of the wonders of God's power and His enduring love. The God who protected Israel watches over you too. Even when there may be little in your life to rejoice about, you can always delight in Him. Give thanks to God. He has not forgotten you—His love endures forever.

DAY 195
True Colors

*May integrity and honesty protect me,
for I put my hope in you.*
PSALM 25:21 NLT

At first the raven appeared solid black, but when she perched in a shaft of sunlight, her feathers shimmered in iridescent emerald, turquoise, and teal: her true colors.

We sometimes hide little acts of dishonesty—taking the bank's pen, pocketing that extra dollar from the clerk's mistake, fudging tax figures. But our integrity is on display at all times to the One who gave His life for us. When our true colors are exposed in the Son-light, we want to shimmer too.

DAY 196
God Saves

*I will give you thanks, for you answered
me; you have become my salvation.*
PSALM 118:21 NIV

A new believer didn't write this verse. The
psalmist thanks God not just for loving Him
enough to tear Him from the claws of original
sin; instead, this mature man of faith recognizes
that God saves him every day, whenever he is
in trouble. God does this in your life too. What
salvation has He worked in your life recently?
What thanks do you need to offer Him now?

DAY 197
Creating a Chalice

"We live by faith, not by sight."
2 CORINTHIANS 5:7 NIV

Okay, so you popped a tire and the boss exploded because you were late for work again. Your dog upchucked in front of the dinner guests. Your daughter failed the big test. Your elderly mother fell and broke her hip. Bill collectors recite your number by heart. That's the outside. On the inside, God is sanding your sharp edges—impatience, frustration, worry—into a smooth chalice filled with His grace.

DAY 198
Eternal Appreciation

LORD my God,
I will praise you forever.
PSALM 30:12 NIV

Even in eternity, you will be thanking God. The appreciation of God's mercy by His people never stops. Without His grace, we would be forever separated from Him, lost in the cares of sin and a hellish existence. The bliss of a heavenly eternity could not be our inheritance.

Could you thank Jesus too much now? Or could you ever find enough words to show Him your love? Maybe it's time to get started on your eternal appreciation of your Lord.

DAY 199
Integrity

"Is not your fear of God your confidence,
and the integrity of your ways your hope?"
JOB 4:6 NASB

"Live your faith." These three little words are the goal of every Christian. Not "Don't smoke, cuss, or chew or hang around with those who do," or even "Be good so you'll get into heaven." Integrity begets behavior, not the other way around. We want to please our Lord by righteous behavior so we can fulfill the challenge of St. Francis of Assisi: "Preach the gospel at all times. Use words if necessary."

DAY 200
Look Ahead to Heaven

*For our light and momentary troubles are
achieving for us an eternal glory
that far outweighs them all.*
2 CORINTHIANS 4:17 NIV

What trouble could you face on earth that will not
seem small in heaven? No pain from this life will
impede you there. Blessing for faithful service to
God will replace each heartache that discourages
you today. When trials and troubles beset you,
look ahead to heaven. Jesus promises you an
eternal reward if you keep your eyes on Him.

DAY 201
Meet Me There

Christ gives me the strength to face anything.
PHILIPPIANS 4:13 CEV

Most women dread going out alone—to restaurants, shopping, social events—even church. Sometimes we are the loneliest when we're in a crowd. It's intimidating to face a roomful of strangers. But it's well worth it to bite the bullet and just go to that church brunch or spiritual retreat or Bible study. I would have missed some awesome blessings if I hadn't gone (alone) to many spiritual events. I found I did know somebody after all. Jesus met me there.

DAY 202
Joy Is Straight Ahead

The genuineness of your faith, being much more precious than gold that perishes, though it is tested by fire, may be found to praise, honor, and glory at the revelation of Jesus Christ.

1 PETER 1:7 NKJV

Trials have a purpose in our lives. As a smith heats up gold to purify it, God heats up our lives to make spiritual impurities rise to the surface. If we cooperate with Him, sin is skimmed off our lives, purifying our faith. Cleansed lives bring glory to God and joy to us. If a trial lies before you today, envision the joy ahead.

DAY 203
Fly Me Away

*But those who hope in the LORD will renew their
strength. They will soar on wings like eagles;
they will run and not grow weary,
they will walk and not be faint.*

ISAIAH 40:31 NIV

On those weary days when our chins drag
the ground, when our feet are stuck fast in
the quagmire of everyday responsibility, this
verse becomes our hope and our prayer. Mount
me up with wings like eagles, Father, fly me away!
Let my spirit soar above the clouds on the winds
of Your strength. Make me strong as a marathon
runner, continuing mile after mile after mile. Be
my tailwind, Lord. Amen.

DAY 204
Greater Ways

For since, in the wisdom of God, the world through wisdom did not know God, it pleased God through the foolishness of the message preached to save those who believe.

1 CORINTHIANS 1:21 NKJV

To this world, God's wisdom doesn't look very wise. Anyone who denies Jesus is blind to the depth of insight God showed in sending His Son to die for us and then raising Him from the dead. But those who accept His sacrifice understand that God's ways are greater than ours and His astuteness far outweighs our own. As His wisdom fills our once-foolish lives, we gain a new perspective on His perception.

DAY 205
Reboot

*Be strong in the Lord
and in his mighty power.*
EPHESIANS 6:10 NLT

The toilet overflows, check bounces, temper flies, scale shows a three-pound gain, kids stampede, husband forgets again. . . .

Ever have one of those days? How marvelous that when we're at our weakest point, our Lord is at His strongest, and He gladly shares that strength with us. He won't necessarily fix the plumbing, but He will reboot our attitudes.

DAY 206
Wise Humility

Woe unto them that are wise in their own eyes,
and prudent in their own sight!

ISAIAH 5:21 KJV

Wisdom without humility isn't wisdom at all. When we feel astute under our own power, we are actually in big trouble and are heading into foolishness! The truly wise person recognizes that all wisdom comes from God, not frail humans. As we tap into His mind and connect with His astuteness, we are wise indeed. There is no one wiser than He.

DAY 207
Fearfully Made

You knit me together in my mother's womb.
I praise you because I am fearfully
and wonderfully made.
PSALM 139:13–14 NIV

Crow's feet, frizzy hair, saddle bags, big feet—most women dislike something about their bodies. We feel much more fearfully than wonderfully made. But God loves us just as we are. He wants us to look past the wrinkles and see laugh footprints; to use those knobby knees for praying and age-spotted hands for serving. And in the process, praise Him for limbs that move, eyes that see, and ears that hear His Word.

DAY 208
Wise Words

*She speaks with wisdom, and faithful
instruction is on her tongue.*

PROVERBS 31:26 NIV

The virtuous woman's mouth speaks kindly
wisdom. Hers is no sharp tongue that destroys
relationships. As we seek to do God's will, truthful
yet caring speech must be ours. Wise words heal
hurting hearts. If we have trouble knowing what
words bring God's healing, we need only to ask
Him to let His Spirit bring wisdom and kindness
to our mouths and tongues. When we speak as
His Spirit directs, we are wise indeed.

DAY 209
Send Me a Sign

Let your unfailing love surround us,
Lord, for our hope is in you alone.
PSALM 33:22 NLT

With deadlines and schedules swirling in my head while driving down the interstate, I did a double take at the car passing me. A white-painted message across the back passenger window grabbed my attention: I am loved. Wow. So am I. It only took a moment to thank Papa God for His unfailing love, but a smile lit my face all day. A simple but profound reminder is all we need from time to time.

DAY 210
Share His Love

I pray that your partnership with us in the
faith may be effective in deepening your
understanding of every good thing
we share for the sake of Christ.
PHILEMON 6 NIV

Many of us have a hard time sharing our faith. So when we hear Paul's encouragement to Philemon, our hearts lift, knowing we aren't the only ones who struggle. Isn't the challenge of witnessing to others worth it once we've read this promise? The salvation of others and our own appreciation of our Lord: Could we have better reasons to share His love?

DAY 211
No Greater Comfort

"O death, where is your victory?
O death, where is your sting?"
1 CORINTHIANS 15:55 NLT

There's no denying that the loss of a loved one stings. Our hearts burn, sear, and ache with pain. But Christ's victory over death after His crucifixion enables His followers to experience that same victory. We too will stand as conquerors of the grave, arm in arm with believers who have gone before us. What greater hope? What greater comfort?

DAY 212

Shine On

*"You are the light of the world.
A town built on a hill cannot be hidden."*
MATTHEW 5:14 NIV

God means you to be a light set where the world can see it clearly—not a hidden flame behind closed doors, with curtains drawn. Being a light isn't always easy—people see everything you do, and they don't always like it. Don't let the critics stop you. Your works were ordained to glorify God, not make people comfortable. Knowing that, are you ready to shine today?

DAY 213
Laugh a Rainbow

"When I see the rainbow in the clouds,
I will remember the eternal covenant between
God and every living creature on earth."
GENESIS 9:16 NLT

Ever feel like a cloud is hanging over your head? Sometimes the cloud darkens to the color of bruises, and we're deluged with cold rain that seems to have no end. When you're in the midst of one of life's thunderstorms, tape this saying to your mirror: cry a river, laugh a rainbow. The rainbow, the symbol of hope that God gave Noah after the flood, reminds us even today that every storm will eventually pass.

DAY 214
Kind Words

Let your speech always be with grace,
seasoned with salt, that you may know
how you ought to answer each one.
Colossians 4:6 nkjv

Your words are a vital part of your witness. Speak to an unbeliever ungraciously, and chances are good that she will never forget it. But study and grow in the Word; then speak wisely and generously to others, and God can use your words to win them to His kingdom. People respond well to kindness and flavorful speech. What are your words saying today?

Asking Why?

God will never forget the needy;
the hope of the afflicted will never perish.
PSALM 9:18 NIV

Why me? Why is God allowing this to happen? Why doesn't He intervene?

When we're in the midst of a difficult time, it's easy to forget that God is not the afflicter, but is the helper and healer of the afflicted. He is not cracking the whip but feels every stripe inflicted on our backs by a sin-filled world—just like those of His only Son, Jesus.

DAY 216
Turn from Wrong

There is therefore now no condemnation to
those who are in Christ Jesus, who do not walk
according to the flesh, but according to the Spirit.
ROMANS 8:1 NKJV

No condemnation! What a wonderful thought for sinners! Forgiven, we know the comfort of having heaven as our ultimate destination. But have we also read the second part of the verse? This is no blanket agreement that okays sin. The joy of our freedom must lead us to turn from all wrong. Our Lord gives the strength to grow in Him.

DAY 217
Tune In

And hope does not put us to shame, because God's love has been poured out into our hearts through the Holy Spirit, who has been given to us.
ROMANS 5:5 NIV

Is your spiritual antenna tuned in to the Holy Spirit? The Holy Spirit is the communicator of the trinity: our helper, comforter, and instructor. Through Him, God pours love and hope into us. Like radio waves broadcasting invisibly through the atmosphere, the Holy Spirit communicates to believers. We must, however, make the effort to tune in our receivers to His frequency and then choose to obey His guidance—even when it's inconvenient.

DAY 218
Inheritors of Earth

*"Blessed are the meek,
for they will inherit the earth."*

MATTHEW 5:5 NIV

In the workplace, meekness isn't often seen as a positive thing. "Looking out for number one" is the theory of many who tout assertiveness as the way to get the most out of life.

But God doesn't say that. Ultimately, those who follow Him faithfully and show their belief to the world will not be the "nice guys" who "finish last" but the inheritors of this earth. What plot of earth might God have mapped out for you?

DAY 219
Saints Preserve Us

*I will always praise you
in the presence of your faithful people.*
PSALM 52:9 NIV

We sing, "Lord, I want to be in that number, when the saints go marching in!" But who exactly are saints? Exceptionally good people like Saint Nicholas or Mother Teresa? The Bible calls all true believers saints. Some think if their derriere simply graces a pew, they're in. But sitting in church no more makes you a Christian than standing in your closet makes you a vacuum cleaner. Only dedicated Christ-lovers will march into heaven. Are you in that number?

DAY 220
Everything for God

Whatever you do, work at it with all your heart,
as working for the Lord.
COLOSSIANS 3:23 NIV

Did you know you are not really working for
your boss? Yes, you report to the one whom your
company hired in that position, but ultimately
you do everything for God, not a man or woman.
So even if your boss isn't great to work for, remind
yourself that you are accountable to Jesus. No
matter who has the position above yours, your
Lord is always in charge of your future.

DAY 221

If You Build It,
He Will Come

*Do not snatch your word of truth from me,
for your regulations are my only hope.*

PSALM 119:43 NLT

Bibles wear and tear. Papers get discarded. Hard drives crash. But memorizing scripture assures us that God's Word will never be lost. His truth will always be at our disposal, any moment of the day or night when we need a word of encouragement, of guidance, of hope. Like a phone call from heaven, our Father communicates to us via scripture implanted in our hearts. But it is up to us to build the signal tower.

DAY 222
Serious Business

Make it your ambition to lead a quiet life:
You should mind your own business
and work with your hands.
1 Thessalonians 4:11 niv

Whether we work at a computer or on a factory production line, those of us who work with our hands shouldn't feel unimportant. Manual labor is serious business in God's sight. Christians who quietly, faithfully go about their business day by day make an important contribution, bearing God's message to a wide range of people. What a testimony our lives become when we live out this verse.

DAY 223
Blameless

*[Jesus] has brought you into his own presence,
and you are holy and blameless as you stand
before him without a single fault.*

<small>COLOSSIANS 1:22 NLT</small>

Holiness. Wouldn't we all like to attain it? But it's impossible. Even if we shave our heads, eat only birdseed, forsake makeup, and wear nothing but mumus, we still wouldn't be holy. We'd just be ugly. The only way we can achieve holiness is through Jesus, who by His death on our behalf ushers us into the presence of God, blameless, beautiful, and whole. And we can leave our mumus at home.

DAY 224
More Than Temporary

Do not be afraid when one becomes rich, when the
glory of his house is increased; for when he dies
he shall carry nothing away; his glory
shall not descend after him.

PSALM 49:16–17 NKJV

This is the Bible's way of saying, "You can't take it with you." When life ends, the only treasures that remain are the works we have done for Jesus. Money and fame cling to earth, soon to be forgotten. So when unbelievers seem to get all the goodies, we just remember that the treasures we send ahead to heaven are greater than any temporary gain.

DAY 225
Whole and Healed

Pray for each other so that you can live together whole and healed. The prayer of a person living right with God is something powerful to be reckoned with.
JAMES 5:16 MSG

Do you have soul siblings? Brothers and sisters in Christ? Caring people who pray for you and with you about, well, everything? Like a life preserver in a turbulent sea, prayer partners are buoyancy for the soul and security through any storm. Heart-bonds, once established, create a trusting environment where we can bare our souls before the Lord in mutual prayer to become whole and healed. Prayer partners are warm hugs from God.

DAY 226
Belong to Jesus

*"If you belonged to the world, it would love you as
its own. As it is, you do not belong to the world,
but I have chosen you out of the world.
That is why the world hates you."*

JOHN 15:19 NIV

Don't expect the world to love you for loving
Jesus. Because He doesn't accept its evil and
neither do you, the world is at enmity with both
of you. That's not such a bad thing. Who would
you rather belong to: Jesus, who holds eternity's
joys in His hands, or the world, which offers so
much sin and pain?

DAY 227
Slathered in SPF

You are my refuge and my shield;
I have put my hope in your word.
PSALM 119:114 NIV

These days, the word *shield* evokes images of glistening sunbathers dotting beaches and carefree children slathered in sunscreen. Like the psalmist's metal shield, sunscreen deflects dangerous rays, preventing them from penetrating vulnerable skin—higher SPF for more protection. When we are immersed in God's Word, we erect a shield that deflects Satan's attempts to penetrate our weak flesh. Internalizing more of God's Word creates a higher SPF: Scripture Protection Factor. Are you well-coated?

DAY 228
A Prayerful Solution

*I want the men everywhere to pray,
lifting up holy hands without
anger or disputing.*
1 TIMOTHY 2:8 NIV

Anger becomes a real trap, even for Christians. When we try to settle differences angrily, we land in big trouble, affecting and even destroying a whole congregation. One solution to anger is prayer. It's hard to stay angry with someone you pray for, even if that person continues to irritate you. As God's Spirit works in your heart, you give the other person a second, a third, or even a hundred and third chance. In Jesus, unrighteous anger cannot linger.

DAY 229
The Foundation and Finale

*I hope to see you soon, and then we will
talk face to face. Peace be with you.*
3 JOHN 14–15 NLT

My prayer is that the message you receive from
this book is that Christ is the ultimate source of
hope. We can live without many things, but we
cannot live without hope. It's the air we breathe,
the water that invigorates every molecule of
our being, the motivation that drives us. Hope
enriches and empowers us, connecting us with
our Papa God. Hope is the essence of our faith.
It's the foundation and the finale.

DAY 230
Letting Go of Anger

Now the works of the flesh are evident,
which are: adultery. . .idolatry, sorcery, hatred,
contentions, jealousies, outbursts of wrath.
GALATIANS 5:19–20 NKJV

It's not something we like to hear, but according to God, anger is right up there with sins such as adultery and idolatry.

Most of us feel wrathful occasionally. But if such feelings take hold of our lives and bitterness results, we fall into sin. When anger touches our reactions, let's use it as a warning sign of an issue that requires our attention. Through wise action and prayer, it need not control us.

DAY 231
Shouts of Joy

He will yet fill your mouth with laughter
and your lips with shouts of joy.
JOB 8:21 NIV

Do you remember the last time you laughed till you cried? For many of us, it's been far too long. Stress tends to steal our joy, leaving us humorless and oh-so-serious. But lightness and fun haven't disappeared forever. They may be buried beneath the snow of a long, wintery life season, but spring is coming, girls. Laughter will bloom again, and our hearts will soar as our lips shout with joy. Grasp that hope!

DAY 232
Today!

*"Therefore do not worry about tomorrow,
for tomorrow will worry about itself.
Each day has enough trouble of its own."*
MATTHEW 6:34 NIV

You can look ahead and obsess about fears for the future or take life one day at a time and enjoy it. But you only live in today, not in the weeks, months, and years that may lie ahead. You can only change life in the moment you're in now. Since worry never improves the future and only hurts today, you'll benefit most from trusting in God and enjoying the spot where He's planted you for now.

DAY 233
I'm No Eeyore

Then [Job's] wife said to him, "Do you still hold
fast your integrity? Curse God and die!"
JOB 2:9 NASB

Job's wife was the unwilling recipient of Satan's attacks because of her husband's righteous life. When the going got tough, our girl lost faith and hope disintegrated. We too sometimes lose sight of all God has done for us and focus only on what He hasn't done. Our optimistic attitudes are consumed by negativity. Job's response is the key to escaping the shackles of Eeyore-ism: "I know that my Redeemer lives" (Job 19:25 NASB).

DAY 234
Sharing with Jesus

Casting all your care upon him;
for he careth for you.
1 PETER 5:7 KJV

You don't have a care in the world that you cannot share—with Jesus, that is. There isn't one thing He doesn't want to hear about from you. Before you ask a friend to pray for you (and you should do that), be certain you share your care with your best Friend, Jesus. Your human friend may try to help you and may do a lot for you, but no one helps like Jesus. There's no worry He can't alleviate or remove.

DAY 235
Confounded Corsets

*Cultivate inner beauty, the gentle,
gracious kind that God delights in.*
1 PETER 3:4 MSG

In our quest for beauty, we buy into all sorts of crazy things: mud facials, cosmetic surgery, body piercings, obsessive dieting, squeezing size 10 feet into size 8 shoes. The image of Scarlett O'Hara's binding corset makes us shudder. (Reminds me of a pair of jeans I wrestled with just last week.) Yet God's idea of beauty is on the inside—where spandex cannot touch. Let's resolve to devote more time pursuing inner beauty that will never require Botox.

DAY 236
Powerful Prayer

"The Lord bless you and keep you; the Lord make his face shine on you and be gracious to you."
NUMBERS 6:24–25 NIV

Want to pray for someone? This is a good way to do it. It's the blessing God gave to Aaron and his sons to pronounce on Israel. What Christian wouldn't appreciate these words, committing her to God's care and wanting her to draw closer to Him? Who would turn down the good things God has to offer? Can you bless your friends and family with these thoughts today?

Good Enough

Leah's eyes were weak, but Rachel
was beautiful of form and face.

GENESIS 29:17 NASB

Have you ever felt like a booby prize? No doubt
Leah did. Hunky Jacob labored seven years
to marry Leah's gorgeous sister, Rachel. Then
their squirrelly father switched his daughters
at the altar. Jacob freaked. Leah tanked. We too
sometimes feel that we're not good enough—that
we don't measure up. But Leah gave birth to six
of the twelve tribes of Israel, the cornerstone of
Judeo-Christendom. God has a mighty plan for
all of us Leahs.

DAY 238
Living for Christ

If you live according to the flesh, you will die;
but if by the Spirit you put to death the
misdeeds of the body, you will live.
ROMANS 8:13 NIV

Living for Christ through His Spirit offers real life, overflowing and abundant. Blessings spill over in obedient lives. But the world, at war with God, doesn't understand. Unbelievers never feel the touch of the Spirit in their hearts and lives, and Jesus' gentle love is foreign to them. Put to death worldly misdeeds, and instead of the emptiness of the world, you'll receive blessings indeed.

DAY 239
A Little Goes a Long Way

*"The LORD our God has allowed a few
of us to survive as a remnant."*
EZRA 9:8 NLT

Remnants. Useless by most standards, but God is in the business of using tiny slivers of what's left to do mighty things. Nehemiah rebuilt the fallen walls of Jerusalem with a remnant of Israel; Noah's three sons repopulated the earth after the flood; four slave boys—Daniel, Shadrach, Meshach, and Abednego—kept faith alive for an entire nation. When it feels as if bits and pieces are all that has survived of your hope, remember how much God can accomplish with remnants!

DAY 240
An Obedient Life

How blessed are those whose way is blameless,
who walk in the law of the LORD.

PSALM 119:1 NASB

Want to be blessed? Then don't live a sin-filled life. God can't pour out blessings on anyone who consistently ignores His commands. Blessings belong to those who hear God's Word and take it to heart, living it out in love. Want to be blessed? Obey the Master. You'll live blamelessly and joyfully.

DAY 241
The SAM Creed

*"If we are thrown into the blazing furnace,
the God whom we serve is able to save
us. . . . But even if he doesn't. . .
we will never serve your gods."*
DANIEL 3:17–18 NLT

Shadrach, Meshach, and Abednego were Israeli boys who were captured and transported as slaves to Babylon. Ordered by their new king to worship his god or die horribly in a fiery furnace, the boys evoked the SAM Creed, an acronym for their names: my God is able to deliver me, but even if He chooses not to, I will still follow Him. Through tough times, let's resolve to live by the SAM Creed.

DAY 242

See Ya, Self

*"Blessed are the poor in spirit,
for theirs is the kingdom of heaven."*
Matthew 5:3 NASB

We don't often think of ourselves as "poor in spirit," but this passage refers to those who are not full of themselves; those who are filled instead with God's spirit. "Poor" in this context means selfless rather than selfish; those with an attitude of dependence on God. How do we become poor in spirit and revel in the hope and promise of heaven? By emptying ourselves of self and the pride of self-sufficiency and refilling ourselves with Jesus.

DAY 243

The Gift of Children

Children are a heritage from the LORD,
offspring a reward from him.

PSALM 127:3 NIV

Today many people see children more as a punishment than a reward. But when you hear of parents who wish they had never had children, you know they're missing out. God creates families to love each other and share His joys. Parents who honestly live out their faith before their children can also guide them into a good family life. Are your children a blessing? He's given them as a reward, not as a punishment. Do you treat them that way?

DAY 244
Cat-i-tude vs. Dog-i-tude

*May those who hope in you not be
disgraced because of me; God of Israel.*
PSALM 69:6 NIV

Are you a hisser or a wagger?

Perhaps you have a feline attitude: it's all about me. I like you for what you can do for me. You'll have my attention only when it's convenient for me. Me, me, me.

Or maybe you have a dog mentality: it's all about you. I love you unconditionally just because you're you. How can I make you happy?

God is glorified by selflessness, not selfishness. Let's strive to make our Master proud.

DAY 245
Wise Correction

A rod and a reprimand impart wisdom, but a child left undisciplined disgraces its mother.
PROVERBS 29:15 NIV

In today's world, fears of child abuse have caused us to ignore this verse. Have we therefore missed the power of correction, which gives our children wisdom? As God restrains us from wrongdoing, we need to stop our children too. We need not touch a child physically to modify behavior. Will we discipline harmful actions now or lose the chance to be proud of our self-controlled children who love the Lord?

DAY 246
Comforting the Comfortless

He brings us alongside someone else who is going through hard times so that we can be there for that person just as God was there for us.
2 CORINTHIANS 1:4 MSG

Heartbroken and hollow after my sixth miscarriage, I struggled to find meaning in my loss. My heavenly Father's arms comforted me when I burst into tears at song lyrics or at the sight of a mother cuddling her infant in WalMart. I finally relinquished my babies to Jesus' loving embrace, confident that I'd see them again one day. I was then able to share His comfort and hope with other women suffering miscarriages.

Reaching Out

*For just as we share abundantly in
the sufferings of Christ, so also our
comfort abounds through Christ.*

2 Corinthians 1:5 niv

Paul knew the pain of persecution, but he also knew the deep comfort God offered. When people gave the apostle trouble, God drew His servant close to His heart. When trials come your way, God will do the same for you. If life is always going smoothly, comfort is meaningless, but when you're in the midst of trouble, He comes alongside with tender love that overflows your trials and reaches out to others.

DAY 248
Loose Lips

We all make many mistakes. For if we could control our tongues, we would be perfect and could also control ourselves in every other way.

JAMES 3:2 NLT

Many of us don't let thoughts marinate long before we spew them out of our mouths. We want to honor God with our speech but seem to spend more time dousing forest fires resulting from sparks kindled by our wagging tongues (James 3:5). Don't despair! There's hope for loose lips! The Creator of self-control is happy to loan us a muzzle (Psalm 39:1) if we sincerely want to change.

DAY 249
Renewal of Faith

"As one whom his mother comforts,
so I will comfort you."
ISAIAH 66:13 NKJV

Like a tender mother, God comforts His people. When life challenges us, we have a place to renew our faith. Instead of questioning God's compassion because we face a trial, we can draw ever nearer to Him, seeking to do His will. Surrounded by His tender arms, we gain strength to go out and face the world again.

DAY 250
The Eyes Have It

All of you together are Christ's body,
and each of you is a part of it.

1 CORINTHIANS 12:27 NLT

Just as our bodies are compiled of many parts, each essential for functioning as a whole, the body of Christ is made up of hands, feet, ears, hearts, and minds. We women understand this concept but tend to compare ourselves to others. If we're hands, we wish we were feet. If we're noses, we'd rather be eyes. Sometimes we feel like bunions. But God views us as equally important, none better than another. Even us toenails!

DAY 251
Giver of Comfort

You ought to forgive and comfort him,
so that he will not be overwhelmed
by excessive sorrow.
2 CORINTHIANS 2:7 NIV

Do you know someone who is sorry for her sin? Then don't keep reminding her of it. If she has sought forgiveness and put it behind her, it is dead. Instead of criticizing, remind her of the power of God that works in her life. Encourage her when temptation calls her name. Then she will not be overcome by sorrow and fall into sin again. Give comfort, and you will be a blessing.

DAY 252
Holding Hands

When I am afraid,
I will put my trust in You.
Psalm 56:3 nasb

While I cowered in a bathroom stall before my first speaking event, my queasy stomach rolled and sweat beaded on my forehead. I prayed for a way to escape. Into my head popped a childhood memory verse: "When I am afraid, I will put my trust in You." My pounding heart calmed. I repeated the scripture aloud and felt my nausea subside and panic diminish. Peace flooded my soul. When we're afraid, Papa God is right beside us holding our hand.

DAY 253
God's Provision

*Now godliness with
contentment is great gain.*
1 TIMOTHY 6:6 NKJV

Paul warned Timothy against false teachers who wanted to use the church for financial gain. If these people were looking for security, they were on the wrong track. Money, which comes and goes, never brings real protection. Our security lies in God's provision. Whether or not we have a large bank account, we can feel content in Jesus. The One who brought us into this world will never forget we require food, clothing, and all the rest. When we truly trust in Jesus, contentment is sure to follow.

DAY 254
Down with Flab

*Workouts in the gymnasium are useful,
but a disciplined life in God is far more so,
making you fit both today and forever.*
1 TIMOTHY 4:7–8 MSG

Do you have Dumbo flaps? You know, those fleshy wings that hang on the underside of your arms when you raise them. A stiff wind could create liftoff. They say regular workouts will tighten those puppies up. . .and significantly reduce wind shear. Just as we exercise muscles to make them strong, we keep our faith in shape by exercising it. Discipline is the way to conquer flab—physically and spiritually!

DAY 255
Contentment in Trouble

The fear of the LORD leads to life: then one rests
content, untouched by trouble.
PROVERBS 19:23 NIV

God doesn't promise we will never suffer trouble, but He does promise something even more important. In the middle of trouble, we will experience real life contentment in the middle of confusion, doubt, or turmoil. Which would you prefer, trouble and life in Jesus or trouble on its own? You can't avoid trouble here on earth. But share life with Him, and contentment will follow.

DAY 256

Bigger Than Fear

Having hope will give you courage. You will be protected and will rest in safety.

JOB 11:18 NLT

Tossing, turning, sleepless nights: What woman doesn't know these intimately? Our thoughts race with the "what ifs" and fear steals our peace. How precious is God's promise that He will rescue us from nagging, faceless fear and give us courage to just say no to anxious thoughts that threaten to terrorize us at our most vulnerable moments. He is our hope and protector. He is bigger than fear. Anxiety flees in His presence. Rest with Him tonight.

DAY 257
Eternal Perspective

"Where, O death, is your victory?
Where, O death, is your sting?"
1 CORINTHIANS 15:55 NIV

Nothing in this world ameliorates the pain of death. Losing one we love reaches deep into our souls. But with His sacrifice, Jesus permanently overcame the sting of mortality. Those who trust in Him do not live for a few short years, but for eternity. When sin takes their lives, they simply move into heaven.

When we lose loved ones, our hearts feel pain. But if they gave their lives to Jesus, He is still victorious. In time we will meet them again in paradise.

DAY 258
Smiling in the Darkness

The hopes of the godless evaporate.
JOB 8:13 NLT

Hope isn't just an emotion; it's a perspective, a discipline, a way of life. It's a journey of choice. We must learn to override those messages of discouragement, despair, and fear that assault us in times of trouble and press toward the light. Hope is smiling in the darkness. It's confidence that faith in God's sovereignty amounts to something. . .something life-changing, life-saving, and eternal.

DAY 259
Death Will Die

The last enemy to be destroyed is death.
1 CORINTHIANS 15:26 NIV

If Jesus conquered death, why do we still suffer with loved ones dying? Because today we live in the promise of death's destruction, not its completion. God's Son has ransomed us through His sacrifice, but death still exists in our world. One day, that will no longer be so. Jesus promises to destroy death entirely—death shall die, and heaven will be ours.

DAY 260
Let Me Be

"Martha. . .you are worried and upset about many things, but few things are needed—or indeed only one. Mary has chosen what is better."
LUKE 10:41–42 NIV

Martha zipped around cleaning, cooking, and organizing. Meanwhile, Mary sat at Jesus' feet. Many of us think like Martha. Will food magically appear on the table? Will the house clean itself? We're slaves to endless to-do lists. Our need to *do* overwhelms our desire to *be*. Constipated calendars attest that we are human doings instead of human beings. But Jesus taught that Mary chose best—simply to be. Lord, help this doer learn to be.

DAY 261
Be Faithful

Good and upright is the LORD;
therefore he instructs sinners in his ways.
PSALM 25:8 NIV

Don't know which way to turn or where to go? God will show you. Just be faithful to Him, and you will hear His still, small voice guiding you; otherwise, circumstances and wise advisers will illuminate the path you need to walk on.

Still doubting? Ask God for forgiveness for sins that bar your communion with Him. Soon, with a clean heart, you'll be headed in the right direction.

DAY 262
Dwelling Place

*Do you not know that you are a temple
of God and that the Spirit
of God dwells in you?*
1 CORINTHIANS 3:16 NASB

Have you ever been awed by the beauty of a majestic cathedral with towering ceilings inlaid with gold and silver, magnificent paintings, rich carpets, and stained glass windows? Only the finest for the house of God Almighty.

Did you know God thinks of you and me as living cathedrals—dwelling places of His Spirit? How amazing to be considered worthy of such an honor! How immeasurable His love to choose us as His dwelling place!

DAY 263
Moving Mountains

"Whoever says to this mountain, 'Be removed and be cast into the sea,' and does not doubt. . .but believes. . .will have whatever he says."
MARK 11:23 NKJV

Don't you wish you had faith like this?

Christians often try to gear up to it, willing it with all their hearts. But that's not what God had in mind. Manipulating Him cannot work.

Only when we fully trust in Him will He move our mountain—even if it's in an unexpected direction.

DAY 264
Brick by Brick

So then faith cometh by hearing,
and hearing by the word of God.
ROMANS 10:17 KJV

Words are powerful. They cut. They heal. They confirm. God uses His Word to help us, to mold us, to make us more like Him. Our faith is built from the bricks of God's Word. Brick by brick, we erect, strengthen, and fortify that faith. But only if we truly listen and hear the Word of God.

DAY 265
Be Prepared

He has also set eternity in the human heart;
yet no one can fathom what God has
done from beginning to end.
ECCLESIASTES 3:11 NIV

Though each of us has a bit of eternity in our hearts, and we cannot rest unless we know the Savior, we also cannot fathom the works of God. That can either make us dissatisfied and doubtful or relaxed, trusting children who know their Father is in control and will care for them from beginning to end. Have you trusted Him who is the Alpha and Omega? Are you prepared for eternity with Him?

DAY 266
Enduring with Grace

*Endurance builds character, which gives us
a hope that will never disappoint us.*
ROMANS 5:4–5 CEV

Heroes come in all packages. My eighteen-year-old niece, Andie, has cerebral palsy and is legally blind. It takes her four times longer than the average person to do just about anything. But she does it anyway: playing drums, walking in leg braces, attending college. Some days, the frustration of being different overwhelms her. But through endurance, she has developed inspiring character traits—rock solid faith, contagious hope, and a stellar sense of humor. When I grow up, I want to be like Andie.

DAY 267
The Christian Life

*Clearly no one who relies on the law
is justified before God, because
"the righteous will live by faith."*

GALATIANS 3:11 NIV

Though some might claim it, crossing all your t's and dotting your i's spiritually does not make you a great Christian. Rules and regulations aren't what the Christian life is about—faith is. Obeying God and following Him as the Spirit leads challenges you to trust Him every moment of your life. With that kind of belief, you'll share His world-changing message.

DAY 268
Small but Mighty

He has. . .exalted the humble.
LUKE 1:52 NLT

God delights in making small things great. He's in the business of taking scrap-heap people and turning them into treasures: Noah (the laughingstock of his city), Moses (stuttering shepherd turned national leader), David (smallest among the big and powerful), Sarah (old and childless), Mary (poor teenager), Rahab (harlot turned faith-filled ancestor of Jesus). So, you and I can rejoice with hope! Let us glory in our smallness!

DAY 269
Our Hearts

Are you willing to recognize, you foolish fellow,
that faith without works is useless?
JAMES 2:20 NASB

Faith isn't faith if actions don't follow belief. No matter what a person says, unless love, compassion, and kindness accompany her words, it would be foolish to consider her Christian testimony believable.

Though works don't save us, they show what's in our hearts. What are we proving by our works today?

DAY 270

I've Got a Name

"I have redeemed you; I have called you
by your name; you are Mine."
ISAIAH 43:1 NKJV

Parents have the indescribable privilege of bestowing a name on their newborn. The identity that little person will be known by for the rest of his or her life. In effect, we give them a part of us. They are an extension of ourselves—our flesh, our blood.

Your heavenly Father has called you by name. He has given you part of Himself: Jesus. You are special to Him. You are His daughter. In this, find security. . .comfort. . .hope.

DAY 271
Shine Brightly

Each one of you also must love his wife as he loves himself, and the wife must respect her husband.
EPHESIANS 5:33 NIV

Marriage is a reciprocal relationship. For it to work well, both parties have to give and receive. If you share house space without the love and respect that make it a home, yours quickly becomes an empty existence. But that's not what God had in mind when He created marriage to reflect His own love for His people. He can help your marriage shine brightly for Him if only you ask Him and are open to His will.

DAY 272
Jets and Submarines

*No power in the sky above or in the earth
below. . .will ever be able to separate us
from the love of God that is revealed
in Christ Jesus our Lord.*

ROMANS 8:39 NLT

Have you ever been diving amid the spectacular
array of vivid color and teeming life in the silent
world under the sea? Painted fish of rainbow hues
are backlit by diffused sunbeams. Multitextured
coral dot the gleaming white sand. You honestly
feel as if you're in another world. But every world
is God's world. He soars above the clouds with us
and spans the depths of the seas. Nothing can
separate us from His love.

DAY 273
The Price of Forgiveness

And according to the law almost all things are purified with blood, and without shedding of blood there is no remission.
HEBREWS 9:22 NKJV

Many people in our world would like cheap forgiveness. They want someone to say they are okay, but they don't want to pay any price for their wrongdoing. That's not what the scriptures say. Remission of sins comes at a high price—sacrificial blood, the blood of Jesus. Jesus says you are worth this expense, and you are clean in Him. Put away sin and rejoice in His deep love for you.

DAY 274
Pick Me Up, Daddy

We boast in the hope of the glory of God.
ROMANS 5:2 NIV

To rejoice means to live joyfully. . .joy-fully
. . .full of joy. Joy is a decision we make. A choice
not to keep wallowing in the mud of our lives.
And there will be mud—at one time or another.
When spiritual rain mixes with the dirt of fallen
people, mud is the inevitable result. The Creator
of sparkling sunbeams, soaring eagles, and
spectacular fuchsia sunsets wants to lift us out
of the mud. Why don't we raise our arms to Him
today?

DAY 275

Pass It On

*"If you forgive others for their
transgressions, your heavenly
Father will also forgive you."*
MATTHEW 6:14 NASB

Forgiveness isn't only something God gives
us. He designed it to be passed on to others.
Doing that, we learn the value of the pardon the
Father offered us. Even when everything in us
screams, "No, I can't forgive," He empowers us
to do so if we trust in Him. Our loving Father
never commands us to actions He cannot also
strengthen us to do.

DAY 276
His Heart's Delight

*The LORD's delight is in those who fear
him, those who put their hope in
his unfailing love.*
PSALM 147:11 NLT

Do you remember how you felt when you witnessed your baby's first faltering steps? Delight. That's what it was. Just like when you heard her sing "Jesus Loves Me" in her squeaky, off-key voice, or she served you tea in tiny pink teacups. The Bible says the Lord delights in us, His children, the very same way. We warm His heart and bring a smile to His lips when we honor Him with our lives. He delights in us.

Importance of Friendship

Do not forsake your friend or a friend of your family, and do not go to your relative's house when disaster strikes you—better a neighbor nearby than a relative far away.

PROVERBS 27:10 NIV

Friendship is important to God, or He would not encourage us to hold fast to it. As Christians, we've known times when other believers seemed closer than our kin. God has brought us into a new family—His own—where faith becomes more important than blood. Through Him our love expands, and we help each other when trouble strikes. No matter where you go, God's people are near.

DAY 278
Rest Stop

*So let's not allow ourselves to get fatigued doing
good. At the right time we will harvest a good
crop if we don't give up, or quit.*
GALATIANS 6:9 MSG

As women, we're used to serving others. It's part
of the feminine package. But sometimes we get
burned out. Fatigued. Overburdened. Girls, God
doesn't want us to be washed-out dishrags, to be
so boggled that we try to pay for groceries with our
frequent shopper card. It's up to us to recognize
the symptoms and rest, regroup, reenergize. This is
not indulgent; it's necessary to do our best in His
name. So, give yourself permission to rest. Today.

DAY 279
Our Best Friend

The righteous choose their friends carefully,
but the way of the wicked leads them astray.
PROVERBS 12:26 NIV

We need friends. But there are those who will lead us into trouble and those who will encourage us and lift us up in our faith, drawing us ever nearer to God. Before we draw near to others, do we consider their spiritual impact on us? If God is our best friend, let us be cautious not to be led astray. When we share friendship with Jesus and our earthly friends, we are truly blessed.

DAY 280
Battle Plan

I sought the LORD, and He answered me,
and delivered me from all my fears.

PSALM 34:4 NASB

There is nothing more wasteful than fear. Fear paralyzes, destroys potential, and shatters hope. It's like an enemy attacking from our blind side. But we don't have to allow fear to defeat us. It's a war that we can win! First comes earnest prayer, then comes change. God will deliver us from our fears if we seek Him and follow His battle plan.

DAY 281
Loving Correction

*For whom the LORD loves He corrects,
just as a father the son in whom he delights.*
PROVERBS 3:12 NKJV

Do you feel the pain of God's correction? Take heart, since it shows He loves you. Just as a loving father will not let his child walk in a dangerous place, your heavenly Father is redirecting you onto another path. Today's discipline may hurt, but in days to come, your sorrow will turn to joy as you reap the blessing that follows obedience. Your Father loves you deeply.

DAY 282
Trumped

And the Lord said to Abraham, "Why did Sarah laugh, saying, 'Shall I indeed bear a child, when I am so old?' Is anything too difficult for the Lord?"

GENESIS 18:13–14 NASB

Sarah, well past menopause and losing the drooping appendage war, was so floored when told of her impending pregnancy that she burst into laughter. How absurd to think those breasts sagging to her navel would nurse a baby! But that's exactly what God had in store. We sometimes forget that God created the systems we consider absolute and impenetrable. He can trump them all with a flick of His pinkie!

DAY 283
He Loves You This Much!

See what great love the Father has lavished on us,
that we should be called children of God!
And that is what we are!

1 JOHN 3:1 NIV

God does not give His love in dribs and drabs.
He lavishes it on us when we come to Him in
faith. All along, He was waiting to make us His
children, and we were the ones who resisted.
But once we face Him as His children, God's love
lets loose in our lives. Nothing is too good for
His obedient children. Praise God that He loves
you that much!

DAY 284
One for All

All of you are part of the same body. There is only one Spirit of God, just as you were given one hope when you were chosen to be God's people.

EPHESIANS 4:4 CEV

Remember the motto of the Three Musketeers? "All for one and one for all." Christ-followers should have the same sense of unity, for we are bound together by eternal hope, the gift of our Savior. Feeling with and for each other, we'll cry tears of joy from one eye and tears of sadness from the other. Loneliness is not an option. Take the first step. Reach out today—someone else's hand is reaching too.

DAY 285
Always Faithful

I will never leave thee, nor forsake thee.
HEBREWS 13:5 KJV

Even when fear or stress challenges you, you need never deal with it single-handedly if Jesus rules your life. When your life seems in shambles around you, He offers strength and comfort for a hurting heart. God never gives up on you. His love cannot change. Today, delight in the One who never deserts you.

DAY 286
They're Just Men

"He may have a great army, but they are merely men. We have the LORD our God to help us and to fight our battles for us!"

2 CHRONICLES 32:8 NLT

When facing attack from an enemy army, Hezekiah uttered these profound words: "They're just men. The God of all creation is standing by to fight for us! No comparison!" And sure enough, against all human reasoning, God sent an angel to defeat the entire enemy army (2 Chronicles 32:21). God still intervenes today to help us fight our battles, whether supernaturally or by natural means. Trust Him. He's got His armor on.

DAY 287

Nothing Is Impossible

"For no word from God will ever fail."
LUKE 1:37 NIV

The angel spoke these words to Mary as he gave her the news that the aged Elizabeth would bear a child. God deals with the impossible in our lives too. We do not bear a Savior, but how has He helped us understand impossible relationships, juggle a hectic schedule, or help a hurting friend? God offers aid, whatever we face. Nothing is impossible for the One at work in our lives. What impossibilities can He deal with in your life? Have you trusted Him for help?

DAY 288
BFF

*I am counting on the LORD; yes, I am counting
on him. I have put my hope in his word.*
PSALM 130:5 NLT

"Best Friends Forever" earn this title of honor
because we've learned we can count on them.
They've proven they'll be there for us through
svelte and bloated, sweet and grumpy, thoughtful
and insensitive. Bailing us out of countless
sinking dinghies, they've held us as we sobbed,
fed our families, watched our kids, and made
us smile. How much more can we count on our
Creator to be there for us?

DAY 289
God Offers Hope

"For I know the plans I have for you," declares the
LORD, *"plans to prosper you and not to harm*
you, plans to give you hope and a future."
JEREMIAH 29:11 NIV

As Judah headed into exile, conquered by a savage pagan people, God offered them hope. He still had a good plan for them, one that would come out of suffering. Their prosperity was not at an end, though their path through hardship had begun.

When God leads you up a rocky path, your hope and future remain secure in Him. Faithful trust is all He asks of you.

DAY 290
Go for It

*When everything was hopeless,
Abraham believed anyway, deciding to
live. . .on what God said he would do.*
ROMANS 4:18 MSG

"You can't do that. It's impossible." Have you ever been told this? Or just thought it because of fear or a previous experience with failure?

This world is full of those who discourage rather than encourage. If we believe them, we'll never do anything. But if we, like Abraham, believe that God has called us for a particular purpose, we'll go for it despite our track records. Past failure doesn't dictate future failure. If God wills it, He fulfills it.

DAY 291
Purposeful Plan

And we know that all things work together for good to those who love God, to those who are the called according to His purpose.

Romans 8:28 nkjv

Life doesn't always look ideal to us. When finances are tight, family problems are serious, or things just don't seem to go our way, we may doubt that God is working in our lives. That's the time we need to reread this verse and take heart. Even things that don't seem good have a purpose in God's plan. As Christians, we can trust in Him even when life is less than perfect.

DAY 292
Heading Home

*We are only foreigners living
here on earth for a while.*
1 CHRONICLES 29:15 CEV

I quivered on the icy Alps peak, more from fear than cold. Which ski slope was my level (beginner) and which were treacherously advanced? A mistake could be deadly. Panic gripped me; I couldn't read the German signs and no one spoke English.

As Christians, we're foreigners on this earth. We don't speak the same language or share the same perspective as nonbelievers. We're only passing through this world on our way to the next. . .heading home.

DAY 293
Open Door

"For God so loved the world that he gave his one and only Son, that whoever believes in him shall not perish but have eternal life."

JOHN 3:16 NIV

These words are God's open door to those who believe in His Son. The barrier between God's holiness and man's sinfulness disintegrates when we believe in Jesus' sacrifice for human sin. But we must walk through that open door with faith to inherit the eternal life God offers. Have you taken that step, or are you still outside the door?

DAY 294
I Do

Let us hold unswervingly to the hope we profess,
for he who promised is faithful.
HEBREWS 10:23 NIV

An important part of any marriage is the vow of faithfulness. We pledge that we will remain faithful to our beloved until death do us part. Faithfulness is crucial to a trusting relationship. We must be able to depend on our spouse to always be in our corner, love us even when we're unlovable, and never leave or forsake us.

God is faithful. We can unswervingly depend on Him to never break His promises.

DAY 295
Gift of Love

The LORD takes delight in his people.
PSALM 149:4 NIV

God doesn't just like you—He delights in you. You are so special to Him; He brought you into His salvation so He could spend eternity with you. God loves each of His children in a special way. You aren't just another in a long line of His people. He knows every bit of you, your faithfulness and failures, and loves each part of you "to pieces." We could never earn such love—it is His special gift to each of us. Let's rejoice in that blessing today.

DAY 296
Unfathomable Grace

Jesus treated us much better than we deserve.
He made us acceptable to God and gave
us the hope of eternal life.
TITUS 3:7 CEV

Whereas justice is getting what we deserve and mercy is not getting what we deserve, grace is getting what we don't deserve. Thankfully, God doesn't automatically dole out justice for our myriad sins, but reaches beyond to mercy and even a step further to grace. As Jean Valjean discovers in the classic story *Les Miserables*, when we truly grasp God's unfathomable mercy and grace, we are then empowered to extend it to others.

DAY 297
God's Love Is at Work

We have known and believed the love that God has for us. God is love, and he who abides in love abides in God, and God in him.

1 JOHN 4:16 NKJV

Trusting in Jesus, you have felt God's love at work in your inner being. The vibrant connection that only Christians experience becomes the center of your life. If you are faithful, His eternal life renews you from head to toe and shines forth vibrantly. Your Spirit-inspired words and actions truly portray God's love to the world.

DAY 298
Roll Down the Window

*"Ask and it will be given to you;
seek and you will find; knock and
the door will be opened to you."*
LUKE 11:9 NIV

Does your fellow have trouble asking directions? Do you cruise about the country on a scenic tour that could have been avoided by asking a simple question? We all find it difficult to some degree when it comes to asking for help. But that's how we reach our final destinations—and not just on the highway. God offers help if we only ask. He's standing there holding the road map. We just have to stop and roll down the window.

DAY 299
Endurance

As you know, we count as blessed those who have persevered. You have heard of Job's perseverance and have seen what the Lord finally brought about. The Lord is full of compassion and mercy.
JAMES 5:11 NIV

Endurance in faith, hard as it may seem, brings happiness. Trials are not a sign of God's disfavor or His will to carelessly punish His children. The tenderhearted Savior never acts cruelly. But through troubles, we draw close to Him and see God's power at work in our lives. Then, like Job, when we persevere in faith, God rewards us bountifully.

DAY 300

A New Tomorrow

Rahab the harlot. . .Joshua spared. . .
for she hid the messengers whom
Joshua sent to spy out Jericho.
JOSHUA 6:25 NASB

Rahab was the unlikeliest of heroes: a prostitute who sold her body in the darkest shadows. Yet she was the very person God chose to fulfill His prophecy. How astoundingly freeing! Especially for those of us ashamed of our past. God loved Rahab for who she was—not what she did. Rahab is proof that God can and will use anyone for His higher purposes. Anyone. Even you and me.

DAY 301
Mercy Triumphs

Mercy triumphs over judgment.
JAMES 2:13 NIV

Not only is God merciful to us, He expects us to pass that blessing on to others. Instead of becoming the rule enforcers in this world, He wants us to paint a picture of the tender love He has for fallen people and to call many other sinners into His love. When we criticize the world and do not show compassion, we lose the powerful witness we were meant to have. As you stand firm for Jesus, may mercy also triumph in your life.

DAY 302
Name Above All Names

O God, we give glory to you all day long and
constantly praise your name.
PSALM 44:8 NLT

So what has God done that deserves our everlasting praise? His descriptive names tell the story: a friend who sticks closer than a brother (Proverbs 18:24 NIV), altogether lovely (Song of Solomon 5:16 NIV), the rock that is higher than I (Psalm 61:2 NIV), my strength and my defense (Isaiah 12:2 NIV), the lifter of my head (Psalm 3:3 AMPC), shade from the heat (Isaiah 25:4 NIV). His very name fills us with hope!

DAY 303
Rebirth and Renewal

He saved us, not because of righteous things we
had done, but because of his mercy. He saved us
through the washing of rebirth and
renewal by the Holy Spirit.

TITUS 3:5 NIV

Could we save ourselves? No way! Even our best efforts fall far short of God's perfection. If God had left us on our own, we'd be eternally separated from Him. But graciously, the Father reached down to us through His Son, sacrificing Jesus on the cross. Then the Spirit touched our lives in rebirth and renewal. Together the three Persons of the Godhead saved us in merciful love.

DAY 304
Feel the Love

*Long before he laid down earth's foundations,
he had us in mind, had settled on us as the focus
of his love, to be made whole and holy by his love.*
EPHESIANS 1:4 MSG

Need a boost of hope today? Read this passage aloud, inserting your name for each "us." Wow! Doesn't that bring home the message of God's incredible, extravagant, customized love for you? I am the focus of His love, and I bask in the hope of healing, wholeness, and holiness His individualized attention brings. You too, dear sister, are His focus. Allow yourself to feel the love today.

DAY 305
God Meets Our Needs

*"He has brought down rulers from their thrones
but has lifted up the humble. He has filled the
hungry with good things but has sent
the rich away empty."*

LUKE 1:52–53 NIV

God provides for every one of His children, even the humblest. Wealth cannot gain His favor nor poverty destroy it. The Father does not look at the wallet, but at the heart. Those who love Him, though they may lack cash, see their needs fulfilled, but unbelievers who own overflowing storehouses harvest empty hearts. God never ignores His children's needs. What has He given you today?

DAY 306
Seeking an Oasis

*He changes a wilderness into a pool of water
and a dry land into springs of water.*
PSALM 107:35 NASB

The wilderness of Israel is truly a barren wasteland—nothing but rocks and parched sand stretching as far as the distant horizon. The life-and-death contrast between stark desert and pools of oasis water is startling.

Our lives can feel parched too. Colorless. Devoid of life. But God has the power to transform desert lives into gurgling, spring-of-water lives. Ask Him to bubble up springs of hope within you today.

DAY 307
He Will Never Fail

*You open your hand and satisfy the
desires of every living thing.*
PSALM 145:16 NIV

Our faithful Lord provides for all His created beings. Will He fail to care for you? How could He satisfy the needs of the smallest birds and beasts yet forget His human child? God is always faithful. Though we fail, He will not. He cannot forget His promises of love and will never forget to provide for your every need.

DAY 308
Forever and Always

*"Never will I leave you;
never will I forsake you."*
HEBREWS 13:5 NIV

Unconditional love. We all yearn for it—from our parents, our spouses, our children, our friends. Love not based on our performance or accomplishments, but on who we are deep down beneath the fluff. God promises unconditional love to those who honor Him. We don't need to worry about disappointing Him when He gets to know us better—He knows us already. Better than we know ourselves. And He loves us anyway, forever and always.

DAY 309
His Gifts

If, by the trespass of the one man, death reigned
through that one man, how much more will
those who receive God's abundant provision of
grace and of the gift of righteousness reign
in life through the one man, Jesus Christ!
ROMANS 5:17 NIV

What greater gift could God give us than His
grace? Once, death ruled over us. Now, life in
Christ commands our days. As we ponder God's
compassion, do we appreciate Christ's sacrifice?
Any spiritual value we have comes from His gifts.
We can never repay Him, but are we living to
show how much we care?

DAY 310
Large and In Charge

"In this world you will have trouble.
But take heart! I have overcome the world."
JOHN 16:33 NIV

"Who's in charge here?" Most mothers have had the experience of returning home to a chaos-wrecked house. Toys, books, clothes, snack wrappers everywhere. "Why isn't [insert correct answer here: your father, the babysitter, Grandma, etc.] in control?"

Our world can sometimes feel chaotic like that. Things appear to be spinning out of control. But we must remember that God is large and in charge. He has a plan.

Knowing God

In the beginning was the Word, and the Word
was with God, and the Word was God.

JOHN 1:1 NIV

Want a picture of God's Word? Look at Jesus, the embodiment of everything the Father wanted to say to us. You can't do that if you don't read the Book that tells of Him.

Maybe that's why God takes it personally when we decide not to read His Word. We're ignoring His tender commands and pushing aside His love. God's scriptures communicate with His children. How can we know Him without His Word?

DAY 312
Only the Best

I have hidden your word in my heart,
that I might not sin against you.
PSALM 119:11 NLT

I adore homemade chicken salad. Honey mustard, sliced grapes, and slivered almonds make it delicious. Quality ingredients produce quality results. It's all poultry, but there's a big difference between white meat and gizzards.

Memorizing scripture is like preparing chicken salad for the soul. God's Word (quality ingredients) will be ready at a moment's notice to guide, comfort, and train us in righteousness (quality results). Anything else is just gizzards.

DAY 313
Flawless Words

"Every word of God is flawless."
PROVERBS 30:5 NIV

Maybe you've had days when you've been tempted to doubt this verse. You wanted to go in one direction, and God's Word said to go in another. But if you were wise, you trusted in its truth instead of following your own way. After all, can you claim that your every word is error-free? No. How much better to follow in the perfect way of your Lord, who willingly shares His wisdom. To avoid many of the faults of this world, trust the flawless Word of God.

DAY 314
Healing Heat

When I am weak, then I am strong.
2 Corinthians 12:10 nasb

As an occupational therapist, I make splints for people with broken bones. The thermoplastic splinting material comes in sheets, hard and unyielding as plywood. When heated, the thermoplastic becomes pliable so it can be cut and molded into a form that promotes healing.

Like that thermoplastic, we're strongest and most usable when we've gone through the melting process. Heat transforms us into moldable beings with which God heals hearts and spirits.

DAY 315
The Light

When Jesus spoke again to the people, he said,
"I am the light of the world. Whoever follows
me will never walk in darkness,
but will have the light of life."

JOHN 8:12 NIV

Following the light of the world means you can see where you're headed. Even when life becomes confusing and totally dark, your goal hasn't changed, and you keep heading in the right direction. Walking in Jesus' light, though you hit a dark patch, you remain on the road with the Savior, and in Him you always see enough to take the next step.

DAY 316

Did You Say Something?

*"Call to Me and I will answer you,
and I will tell you great and mighty
things, which you do not know."*

JEREMIAH 33:3 NASB

As someone who's been there, done that, you've gotta love the commercial where the husband has his face buried in the newspaper when his wife pops the no-win question: "Does this dress make me look fat?" "You bet," he distractedly replies.

God promises to not only hear us when we call to Him, but to answer by teaching us new and amazing things. He's never distracted. He's always listening. And He always cares.

DAY 317
Hope in Him

Put your hope in God, for I will yet praise him,
my Savior and my God.
PSALM 42:5–6 NIV

Where else should the believer place her hope? No human has power to turn her life around without Jesus. No solution lies beyond Him, and He never pushes her away. When the world becomes harsh, she still receives His gentle encouragement.

Though you wait long and the path seems hard, hold on to Jesus. Words of praise will pass your lips as you see His salvation accomplished. Your God will never let you fall.

DAY 318
It's Not Over

When the wicked die, their hopes die with them,
for they rely on their own feeble strength.
PROVERBS 11:7 NLT

Tony Dungy, Super Bowl champion, coach, and author of *Quiet Strength*, said, "It's because of God's goodness that we can have hope, both for here and the hereafter."

Coach Dungy's testimony of eternal hope for those who rely on God's infinite strength touched many hearts after the tragic loss of his teenage son. Death is not the end. There is a hope, a future for those who choose to not rely on their own feeble strength.

Be Strong

Be strong and take heart,
all you who hope in the LORD.
PSALM 31:24 NIV

Hope is not some weak, airy-fairy kind of thing. It takes strength to put your trust in God when life batters your heart and soul. Weaklings rarely hold on to positive expectation for long because it takes too much from them. But the spiritually strong put their trust in God and let Him lift up their hearts in hope. Then battering may come, but it cannot destroy them. Hope makes Christians stronger still.

DAY 320
Streets of Treats

*What you hope for is kept
safe for you in heaven.*
COLOSSIANS 1:5 CEV

Heaven. Will the streets really be paved with gold? Or even better—chocolate? No, if our earthly treasures are our source of security and hope, we're in trouble. Rust, thieves, decay, recession. . . things just aren't safe. But peace? Joy? Reveling forever in our Lord's presence? All waiting for us safely in heaven. (But who says we can't hope for Godiva-cobbled streets?)

DAY 321
Obedience = Joy

"I have told you this so that my joy may be in you and that your joy may be complete."
JOHN 15:11 NIV

What wouldn't we do to share Jesus' complete joy! But this verse comes after one of Jesus' commands to obedience. Ah, now do we change our minds? Does joy suddenly become impossible? When Jesus calls us to act, do we follow, or do we decide it's too hard and give up immediately? Let's keep our eyes on the outcome—the joy of our Lord filling our lives. Then obedience too may become a joy.

DAY 322
Justice for All?

Our God, you save us, and your fearsome deeds answer our prayers for justice!
PSALM 65:5 CEV

It's not fair! How many times have we uttered this indignant cry when life handed us injustice? We demand justice—it's what we deserve, right? But what about all those times we've misstepped or misjudged? James 2:13 tells us that mercy triumphs over justice. Mercy forgives mistakes and doesn't dole out what is deserved. Mercy—like a jail sentence pardoned. Mercy—like a man on a cross.

DAY 323
Joy Will Come

My lips will shout for joy when I sing praise to you—I whom you have delivered.
PSALM 71:23 NIV

Having trouble finding joy in your life today? Do what the psalmists often did and remind yourself what God has already done for you. How many ways has following Him blessed you? Begin by thanking Him for His saving grace, and the joy starts, no matter what you face today. Your lips will show the delight in your heart.

DAY 324
Smiling Hearts

*Weeping may last for the night,
but a shout of joy comes in the morning.*
PSALM 30:5 NASB

What woman hasn't seen the dim underbelly of
2 a.m. through hot tears? God gave us emotionally
sensitive spirits and is willing to sit with us as we
weep through the long, hard night. Sometimes
"night" lasts for a season. But He promises that
the sun will eventually rise. And on that glorious
morning, we'll be filled with so much joy, even
our hearts will smile. Joy is appreciated most in
the wake of disappointment.

DAY 325
Close to Jesus

"Be still, and know that I am God."
PSALM 46:10 NIV

So often, we seek to do things for God or to prove our Christian witness. But if we become simply caught up in busyness, we lose the distinction of our faith: a close relationship with Jesus. Knowing God is not about what we do, but whom we love. Our good works mean little if we disconnect from Him. Spend time being still with God today, and a deepened knowledge of Him will be your blessing.

DAY 326
Who's Your Daddy?

His name is the LORD.
A father to the fatherless.
PSALM 68:4–5 NIV

His father left when my friend Ben was two.
Ben recognized him once—from pictures—at
a family funeral, but his father intentionally
turned away. When Ben was thirty-five, with a
family of his own, his father suddenly showed up,
seeking a relationship. Sadly, he was diagnosed
with cancer shortly after their reunion and died
within one year. Ben mourned but knew his real
paternal relationship was with God, the Father
to the fatherless.

DAY 327
Know Him Intimately

*"I will take you as my own people, and I will be
your God. Then you will know that I am the
LORD your God, who brought you out from
under the yoke of the Egyptians."*
EXODUS 6:7 NIV

God freed the Hebrews from slavery and brought
them to their new land. But He didn't stop
there. Today He still proves Himself to people
by freeing them from sin's slavery and creating
loving relationships with them. Has God freed
you from sin? Then know Him intimately. Draw
near and enjoy His blessings, no matter what
"slavery" you've faced before.

DAY 328
Fresh and Green

They will still bear fruit in old age,
they will stay fresh and green.
PSALM 92:14 NIV

Doris, a tiny ninety-year-old widow in my Bible study, is teaching me how to be a blessing. That's her prayer every morning of her life: Lord, make me a blessing to someone today. And sure enough, God uses her to touch lives in His name—helping a frantic woman find her lost keys; taking a sick neighbor to the doctor; offering a friendly word to the grumpy, wheelchair-bound man. Little blessings are big indeed to those in need.

Father and Son

We know also that the Son of God has come and has given us understanding, so that we may know him who is true. And we are in him who is true by being in his Son Jesus Christ. He is the true God and eternal life.

1 JOHN 5:20 NIV

How do we know God? Through His Son, Jesus, who helps us understand the love of His Father. There is no space, no difference of opinion, between Father and Son. When we know the Son, we know God truly. Trust in one is trust in both.

DAY 330
Superwoman Isn't Home

*"But we will devote ourselves to prayer
and to the ministry of the word."*
ACTS 6:4 NASB

As busy women, we've found out the hard way that we can't do everything. Heaven knows we've tried, but the truth has found us out: Superwoman is a myth. So we must make priorities and focus on the most important. Prayer and God's Word should be our faith priorities. If we only do as much as we can do, then God will take over and do what only He can do. He's got our backs, girls!

DAY 331
Perfecting Our Love

Jesus replied: " 'Love the Lord your God
with all your heart and with all your
soul and with all your mind.' "
MATTHEW 22:37 NIV

This simple command can be a real challenge, can't it? No matter how we try, in our own power, to love God completely, we always seem to fail somewhere. Only as God's Spirit works in our hearts will our whole being become ever more faithful. God works in us day by day, perfecting our love. Ask Him to help you love Him today.

DAY 332
He Is Able

The prospect of the righteous is joy.
PROVERBS 10:28 NIV

Living joyfully isn't denying reality. The righteous do not receive a "Get Out of Pain Free" card when they place their trust in Christ. We all have hurts in our lives. Some we think we cannot possibly endure. But even in the midst of our darkest times, our heavenly Father is able to reach in with gentle fingers to touch us and infuse us with joy that defies explanation. Impossible? Perhaps by the world's standards. Yet He is able.

DAY 333
Gentle Reminder

If a man say, I love God, and hateth his brother,
he is a liar: for he that loveth not his brother
whom he hath seen, how can he love
God whom he hath not seen?

1 JOHN 4:20 KJV

John's letter surely knows how to challenge us. Now we wonder, *Do I love God at all?* Surely, on our own, we couldn't. But when we accept God and receive His love, our attitude changes. In Jesus we can love even a bothersome brother. Sometimes we just need a gentle reminder.

DAY 334
Lighthouse Love

For God, who said, "Light shall shine out of darkness," is the One who has shone in our hearts.
2 CORINTHIANS 4:6 NASB

Have you heard the story of the lighthouse keeper's daughter who kept faithful vigil for her sailor? Every night she watched as the light's beam pierced the blackness and sliced through raging storms, driven by relentless hope that her lover would return to her on the morning's tide. God loves us like that. He's our light in the darkness: guiding, beckoning, and filling our hearts with hope. He never tires. He never stops.

DAY 335
New Life

*Therefore, if anyone is in Christ, he is a new
creation; old things have passed away;
behold, all things have become new.*
2 Corinthians 5:17 nkjv

New life in Christ: what indescribable freedom to be separated from our sin! No longer bound by it but able to live in Him, we joyfully race into our new existence.

But in time, our tendency to fall into sin tarnishes God's gift. Suddenly, we don't feel so new. "Old" Christians need only turn again to Christ for forgiveness, and the Spirit's cleansing makes us new again.

DAY 336
That Morning

*You have placed your faith and hope in
God because he raised Christ from the
dead and gave him great glory.*
1 PETER 1:21 NLT

Have you ever wondered how Mary felt that
Easter morning when she discovered Jesus' tomb
empty? Already grieving, imagine the shock of
discovering the body of her Savior—the One
who held all her hopes and dreams—gone! How
can that be? Maybe. . . ? Hope glimmers. But
no—impossible. He did say something about
resurrection, but that was figurative, wasn't it?
*Who are. . . You are? I must run and tell them. It's
true! He has risen! He's alive! My hope lives too!*

DAY 337

Celebrate Your Newness

*If Christ is in you, the body is dead
because of sin, but the Spirit is life
because of righteousness.*

ROMANS 8:10 NKJV

Know Jesus? Then your body and your fleshly desires are less important than your spirit. Because Jesus lives in you, sin has no permanent claim on your life. Though it tempts you and you may give in for a time, it no longer has a firm grasp on all your days. You can turn aside from it and dwell in your Lord instead. Celebrate your newness in Jesus: live for Him today!

DAY 338
Walkin' Boots

I heard about you from others;
now I have seen you with my own eyes.
JOB 42:5 CEV

As children we sang, "Jesus loves me, this I know; for the Bible tells me so," and we believed because, well, we were told to. But we reach a crossroads as adults: either pull on the boots of faith and take ownership or simply polish them occasionally—maybe at Easter and Christmas— and allow them to sit neglected and dusty in the closet. Have you taken ownership of your faith? Go ahead, sister, those boots were made for walkin'!

DAY 339
Don't Be Afraid to Ask

Brothers and sisters, pray for us.
1 THESSALONIANS 5:25 NIV

Do you find it hard to ask others to pray for you? Don't be afraid to take that step into humility. Paul wasn't when he asked the Thessalonians to pray for his ministry. Being part of the church requires an interdependence of prayers given and received. As a congregation prays for each other, their spirits connect in a new, caring way. Choose carefully those with whom you share private concerns, but never fear to ask a mature Christian to pray for you.

DAY 340
Labor

We call to mind your work of faith, your labor of love, and your patience of hope in following our Master, Jesus Christ, before God our Father.
1 Thessalonians 1:3 msg

Labor. The word alone draws a shudder from the most stalwart of pregnant women. Just as laboring to bring forth new physical life requires patience, birthing new spiritual life may require an intensive labor of love: ceaseless prayer. Countless women on their knees praying for the salvation of a loved one have rejoiced in answered prayer. Their secret? Patience of hope.

DAY 341
The Best Answer

Pray without ceasing.
1 THESSALONIANS 5:17 KJV

Haven't gotten an answer to your prayer? Don't give up. There's no time limit on speaking to God about your needs. It's just that we often work on a different time schedule from God. We want an answer yesterday, while He has something better in mind for tomorrow. So keep praying. God listens to His children and gives them the best answer, not the fastest one.

DAY 342
Essential Trio

Love is patient, love is kind.
1 CORINTHIANS 13:4 NIV

Love, patience, and kindness go together. In fact, it's hard to imagine love that would not express itself in both patience and kindness! That's because even intense, God-sent love for the people in your life does not protect you from feeling annoyed with them or exasperated by their actions from time to time. Yet true love prompts you to respond with patience, not intolerance, as they struggle through their weaknesses. True love compels you to treat them with kindness, not malice, when they upset or offend you. Love, patience, kindness—three must-haves for strong, healthy, and lasting relationships

Blessing Behind Repentance

*"Repent, then, and turn to God, so that your sins
may be wiped out, that times of refreshing
may come from the Lord."*

ACTS 3:19 NIV

When we consider repentance, we tend to think
it's hard. That's only because we're shortsighted.
Giving up sin may not appeal to our hardened
hearts because we're not looking at the blessing
set behind repentance. Yet as we turn from sin,
we feel the refreshing breath of God's Spirit
bringing new life to our lives. Then, does anything
seem difficult?

DAY 344
Wait Just a Minute

We wait in hope for the LORD;
he is our help and our shield.
PSALM 33:20 NIV

Impatience: archenemy of women. Like Batman's Riddler or Superman's Lex Luthor, impatience stalks us, plots our demise, and blindsides us via thoughtless neighbors, inconsiderate drivers, careless clerks, dense husbands, children taking *for–ev–er*. But waiting is an unavoidable part of life, and the Bible says we don't have to be undone by it. The Lord's patience is our shield and defense, and He's got plenty stockpiled.

DAY 345

In His Power

*I can do all things through
Christ who strengthens me.*
PHILIPPIANS 4:13 NKJV

Need strength? Turn to God for all you need.
Why take on life by yourself when He offers
all you need? Often, as obedient Christians,
we make great efforts with our feeble spiritual
muscles. But ultimately our own strength always
fails. When Christ's Spirit works through us, the
Christian life flows smoothly; in His power we
accomplish His purposes. Today, is Christ bearing
the burden or are we? Only He has the might we
need in our lives.

DAY 346
Sprouts

*"For there is hope for a tree, when it is cut down,
that it will sprout again."*

JOB 14:7 NASB

Have you ever battled a stubborn tree? You know, one you can saw off at the ground but the tenacious thing keeps sprouting new growth from the roots? You have to admire the resiliency of that life force, struggling in its refusal to give up. That's hope in a nutshell, sisters. We must believe, even as stumps, that we will eventually become majestic, towering evergreens if we just keep sending out those sprouts.

DAY 347

You Will Prosper

*"But you shall meditate in it [the Book of
the Law] day and night. . .do not turn
from it. . .that you may prosper."*
JOSHUA 1:8, 7 NKJV

God promised success to Joshua if he obeyed
His Word. That promise works for you too. But
sometimes you may not feel that obeying God
has brought you great prosperity. Just wait. It
may take time, the success may not take the
form you expect, or you may not see the results
until you reach heaven, but God will prosper
those who do His will. He promised it, and His
promises never fail.

DAY 348

Getting to Know You

For the law never made anything perfect.
But now we have confidence in a better hope,
through which we draw near to God.

Hebrews 7:19 nlt

Following Old Testament law used to be considered the way to achieve righteousness, but obeying rules just doesn't work for fallible humans. We mess up. We fail miserably. Then Jesus came and provided a better way to draw near to God. He bridged the gap by offering us a personal relationship rather than rules. Together we laugh, cry, love, grieve, rejoice. We get to know our Papa God through our personal relationship with Him.

DAY 349
Real Success

*Save now, we beseech You, O Lord; send now
prosperity, O Lord, we beseech You,
and give to us success!*
PSALM 118:25 AMPC

Is it wrong to pray for success? No. But notice that the Bible connects success to God's salvation. Prosperity or any other achievement means little when it's separated from God's will and our obedience to Him. When you ask to attain something, do you also seek God's saving grace in that part of your life? If so, you'll have real success—spiritual and temporal blessings.

DAY 350

Nothing More Than Feelings

LORD, sustain me as you promised, that I may live! Do not let my hope be crushed.
PSALM 119:116 NLT

Whatever our foe—unemployment, rejection, loss, illness—we may feel beaten down by life. Hope feels crushed by the relentless boulder bearing down on our souls. We feel that we can't possibly endure another day. Yes, we feel, we feel. But feelings are often deceiving. God promises to sustain us, to strengthen us, so that we might withstand that massive rock. We can trust Him. He will not allow us to be crushed!

DAY 351
Lean on Jesus

*"Therefore if the Son makes you free,
you shall be free indeed."*
JOHN 8:36 NKJV

Sometimes we don't feel freed from sin. Temptations draw us even though we love Jesus. So, His words here can be both comforting and challenging. The Jews wanted to trust in their spiritual history, not God. That plan didn't work well for them, and it won't work for us either. We can't rely on history or our past deeds to put sin behind us. What will work? Leaning on Jesus every day, trusting Him to make us free indeed!

DAY 352
Redeemed!

O Israel, hope in the LORD; for with the LORD there is lovingkindness, and with Him is abundant redemption.
PSALM 130:7 NASB

The psalmist knew Israel had a rotten track record. Throughout Old Testament history, God miraculously delivered the Israelites from trouble repeatedly, and they would gratefully turn to Him, only to eventually slip again into rebellion and more trouble. Sounds a lot like you and me, doesn't it? But thankfully, ours is a redemptive God; a God who offers abundant loving-kindness and forgiveness. A God of second chances—then and now.

DAY 353

Appreciation Overflow

Continue to live your lives in [Jesus], rooted and built up in him, strengthened in the faith as you were taught, and overflowing with thankfulness.
COLOSSIANS 2:6–7 NIV

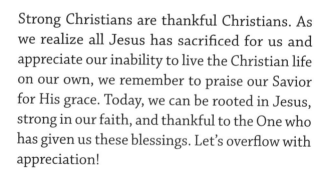

Strong Christians are thankful Christians. As we realize all Jesus has sacrificed for us and appreciate our inability to live the Christian life on our own, we remember to praise our Savior for His grace. Today, we can be rooted in Jesus, strong in our faith, and thankful to the One who has given us these blessings. Let's overflow with appreciation!

DAY 354

Mr. Clean for the Soul

As far as the east is from the west, so far has
He removed our transgressions from us.
PSALM 103:12 NASB

Dirty little secrets. We all have them. Exposing them is a popular theme for television shows these days. But we don't have to wallow in the muck of our past. God has promised to wash us clean of our dirty little secrets and remove them as far as the east is from the west when we repent of our wrongdoings and ask him for forgiveness. An immaculate and sparkling fresh start—redemption is Mr. Clean for the soul!

DAY 355
Wonderful Thanks

Oh, give thanks to the LORD, for He is good!
For His mercy endures forever.
PSALM 136:1 NKJV

Now, honestly, how do you respond to this call for thanks? Does your heart leap at the opportunity, or does it just hit you with a dull thud? Why is it so important to thank God? Because He will always be merciful to you. Whether you rejoice easily or hit the floor with a thud, if you have trusted in the Savior, He still loves you. Isn't that something wonderful to give thanks for?

DAY 356

Counting on It

Blessed is the one who perseveres under trial,
because, having stood the test, that person
will receive the crown of life that the Lord
has promised to those who love him.

JAMES 1:12 NIV

Some think that when you turn your life over to Christ, troubles are over. But if you've been a believer for more than a day, you'll realize that the Christian life is no Caribbean cruise. There will be trials; there will be tribulations. Count on it. But Jesus promises a glorious reward for our perseverance through those hard times. Count on that even more.

DAY 357
God Calls Us to Joy

Consider it pure joy, my brothers and sisters,
whenever you face trials of many kinds.

JAMES 1:2 NIV

Joy? To be faced with trials should cause us joy? Hard to imagine, isn't it? But God calls us to joy when unbelievers persecute us because of our faith or when our situation is merely difficult. It is a joy to Him that we have stood firm in faith, and He calls us to share His delight. That doesn't mean we seek out trials, but that we face the situation hand in hand with God. In trials, our spiritual strength increases.

DAY 358
Overflowing Love

Precious in the sight of the LORD
is the death of His godly ones.
PSALM 116:15 NASB

Jesus wept. Two small words that portray the enormity of Jesus' emotion following the death of His dear friend, Lazarus (John 11:35). Jesus knew Lazarus wouldn't stay dead, that he'd soon miraculously rise from the grave. So why did Jesus weep? The depth of His love for those precious to Him overflowed. Our Lord grieves with us in our losses today and comforts us with the knowledge that His beloved will rise to eternal life in heaven.

DAY 359
His Concern

The righteous cry out, and the LORD hears,
and delivers them out of all their troubles.
PSALM 34:17 NKJV

As God's child, you have His ear 24/7 if only you will pray. Every need, trouble, or praise is His concern. And not only will He hear about your trials, He will deliver you from them. Feel discouraged in your troubles? You need not stay that way. Just spend time with Jesus. His help is on the way.

DAY 360
Guilt-Free

*"I will forgive their wickedness,
and I will never again remember their sins."*
HEBREWS 8:12 NLT

Guilt. It tends to consume us women to the point that 90 percent of the things we do are motivated by guilt. But God says we don't have to allow guilt to control us. We should learn from past mistakes, certainly, and then shed the guilt like a moth-eaten winter coat. Don a fresh spring outfit and look ahead. Our past prepares us for the future if we are open to the present.

God's Compassionate Salvation

*Do not repay anyone evil for evil. Be careful to
do what is right in the eyes of everyone.*

ROMANS 12:17 NIV

Tit-for-tat retribution for evil is not a principle
of our compassionate God. We understand this
if we've received His undeserved salvation. With
such a gift, God has opened our hearts to treating
our enemies as He has treated us. If we fail to
count up each wrong and repay it with harshness,
lost souls may understand God's compassionate
salvation. By doing right, even when we receive
wrong in return, we become powerful witnesses.

DAY 362
Close to You

I stay close to you, and your powerful
arm supports me.
PSALM 63:8 CEV

There's an old saying: "I used to be close to God, but someone moved." If God is the same yesterday, today, and tomorrow, He's not the one going anywhere. So how do we stay close to God? So close that His powerful arm supports, protects, and lifts us up when we're down? Prayer: as a lifestyle, as much a part of ourselves as breathing. Prayer isn't just spiritual punctuation; it's every word of our life story.

DAY 363
A Real Gift

*"Believe in the Lord Jesus,
and you will be saved."*

ACTS 16:31 NIV

A genuine gift doesn't cost you a cent. It's given to you because the giver loves you and wants to make you happy. Who would insult such a gracious person by pulling out money to pay for the gift? Yet that's what happens when godly acts are done to earn salvation! It's trying to pay for the gift of love God has given to you solely because He delights in you and desires to fill your heart with joy. Doing good—not to earn His gift but to thank Him for it—provides your Spirit-given motivation for your many kindnesses to others.

DAY 364
Raising Our Hopes

*"Did I ask you for a son, my lord?" she said.
"Didn't I tell you, 'Don't raise my hopes'?"*
2 KINGS 4:28 NIV

Are you afraid to raise your hope in God's provision for fear that hope will crash and burn? The woman from Shunem had everything but her heart's desire—a child. She was afraid to believe Elisha's prediction of her pregnancy, but his prayerful intervention made her dream come true. When the boy later died, however, she lashed out. God restored her son and raised her hope from the dead. Literally. Dare we raise our hopes too?

DAY 365
Source of Salvation

*He became the source of eternal
salvation for all who obey him.*
HEBREWS 5:9 NIV

Salvation in Jesus is important to our earthly lives. How many times has He dispelled danger or helped us avoid it? How often has sin failed to mar our lives because we obeyed His commands? But Jesus is also the source of salvation in eternity. Instead of remaining forever in our earthly lives, God planned to bring us into everlasting life with Him, in His restored kingdom. In heaven, we will praise His salvation, without end.

SCRIPTURE INDEX

DAILY INSPIRATION FOR A WOMAN'S SPIRIT!

Peace and Comfort for Difficult Times
Infuse your spirit with peace and comfort in this wonderfully uplifting devotional created just for you. One reading for every day of the year will bring much-needed assurance to your soul.

Paperback / 978-1-64352-883-0 / $9.99

Daily Prayers and Promises for Women
Daily Prayers and Promises for Women features 365 devotional prayers that touch on many practical topics important to women—such as Beauty, Family, Loneliness, and Trust. Each prayer is complemented by an encouraging scripture.

Paperback / 978-1-64352-849-6 / $9.99